Happiness Mountain
MAKE EVERY EXPERIENCE A HAPPY EXPERIENCE

AMAL INDI

Copyright © 2023 Amal Indi

First Edition, August 2023

Paperback ISBN: 978-1-7340687-7-1

Library of Congress Control Number: 2021901135

All rights reserved.

No part of this book may be reproduced or transmitted without written permission, except for brief quotations in reviews and noncommercial uses permitted by copyright law.

For permissions or bulk orders:

Email: support@happinessmountain.com

General Disclaimer

The content in this book is for informational purposes only. The author and publisher disclaim all liability for any loss or injury resulting from the use of this book.

Medical Disclaimer

This book is not a substitute for professional medical advice, diagnosis, or treatment. Always consult with a qualified healthcare provider for medical advice. The author and publisher are not responsible for any adverse effects or consequences from the use of information in this book. The information presented in this book is based on the author's research and personal experiences and is not intended to replace medical advice from qualified healthcare professionals.

Published by Happiness Mountain Inc.

Website: www.happinessmountain.com

For my parents,
Mahipala and Chitra Indigahawela,

CONTENTS

INTRODUCTION: WHAT IS HAPPINESS?

1. Happiness Definition — 3
2. Happiness Methodology — 14
3. Happiness Philosophy — 23
4. Four Quadrants Of Happiness — 27
5. Reprogramming Your Mind for Happiness — 30

HAPPINESS EXPERIENCE ONE: LIVING WITH FULL POSITIVE ENERGY

6. Eight Positive Power-Ups: Keys to Positive Energy — 37
7. Gratitude Power-Up — 42
8. Uplift Power-Up — 47
9. Love Power-Up — 53
10. Acceptance Power-Up — 60
11. Patience Power-Up — 65
12. Moderation Power-Up — 69
13. Mindfulness Power-Up — 74
14. Integrity Power-Up — 83

HAPPINESS EXPERIENCE TWO: LIVING WITHOUT STRESS OR WORRY

15. Eight Thought Bugs®: Triggers of Negative Energy — 91
16. How to Spot and Stop Thought Bugs® — 97
17. Worry Thought Bug — 105
18. Anger Thought Bug — 113
19. Expectation Thought Bug — 121
20. Craving Thought Bug — 125
21. Judgmental Thought Bug — 131
22. Fear Thought Bug — 137

23. Self-Limiting Thought Bug	143
24. Do-it-Later Thought Bug	154

HAPPINESS EXPERIENCE THREE:
LIVING A JOYFUL AND BALANCED LIFE

25. Four Happy Hormones: Daily DOSE	163
26. How to Create a Joyful & Balanced Life	168
27. Dopamine = Motivation + Drive + Pleasure	180
28. Oxytocin = Bond + Trust + Love	188
29. Serotonin = Elevated Mood + Self-Esteem	194
30. Endorphins = Healing + Well-being	200
31. Feeding Happy Hormones in Unhealthy Ways PART	206

HAPPINESS EXPERIENCE FOUR:
LIVING WITH INNER HAPPINESS

32. How to Gain Inner Happiness	215
33. Connect to Your Higher Self	223

HAPPINESS EXPERIENCE FIVE:
FIND YOUR GREATNESS

34. How to Discover Your Greatness	237
35. Your Nine Givebacks	242

HAPPINESS EXPERIENCE SIX:
LIFE FULFILLMENT

36. How to Attain Fulfillment	251
37. Use the Power of Your Mind	261
38. Use the Power of Energy	277

CONCLUSION:
MAKE THE WORLD A HAPPIER PLACE

39. Living on Happiness Mountain	293

Notes	297
Acknowledgments	299
About the Author	301
Also by Amal Indi	303
Happiness Mountain App	305

Introduction: What is Happiness?

CHAPTER 1
HAPPINESS DEFINITION

Happiness is the most important experience that we as human beings seek throughout our entire lives. Yet, there is no clear definition of happiness in the world today.

How can we expect to be happy to the fullest if we do not know what happiness is? To better understand what people perceive as happiness, I asked, "What does happiness mean to you?" The following are a few answers from the survey:

- "Peace of mind."
- "Joy, well-being, peace, love, family, friendship."
- "Being able to spend time doing what I love, freedom, goals, learning and growing."
- "Lack of negative things, lack of worries in the moment, contentment."
- "Money."
- "Happiness is different for everyone. It is a feeling."

Now, let's look at the definition of happiness in the Merriam-Webster dictionary:

***happiness* n.**[1]
1 a: a state of well-being and contentment, joy
b: a pleasurable or satisfying experience
I wish you every happiness in life.
I had the happiness of seeing you (W. S. Gilbert)
2: felicity, aptness
A striking happiness of expression
3: (obsolete) good fortune; prosperity
All happiness bechance to thee (William Shakespeare)

Based on my life experiences and what others say about happiness, including the dictionary definitions, I realized that I needed a practical definition for happiness that I could understand and follow.

Everyone has happy moments in life. Suppose you are awake sixteen hours a day after eight hours of sleep—how much time are you truly happy in these sixteen hours?

- If you are happy only 20 percent of your day, you will not feel truly happy in life.
- If you are happy 50 percent of your day, you will feel like you have an OK life.
- If you are happy 60 percent or above, you are living a happy life.
- If you are happy 80 percent and above, you're living a phenomenally happy life.

What if you could change the times that you are not happy to happy moments?

If you want to get better at something, you must study and become proficient in that subject. You do not know what you are missing if you do not learn. The same principle applies to happiness. If you want to be happier, study what happiness is. If happiness is important to you, master it.

UNDERSTANDING CONSCIOUS VS. ACCIDENTAL HAPPINESS

By understanding happiness, you can consciously live a happier life. Without this knowledge, you might still find moments of happiness, but it's more like "accidental happiness." On the other hand, when you grasp the true meaning of happiness, you're practicing "conscious happiness." Here are its advantages:

- When unhappiness strikes, you quickly know the way back to joy and minimize the time you live in unhappy suffering.
- You can prevent going into unhappiness.
- If you're already happy, you can amplify it and maintain that uplifting feeling consistently.
- You can spread this happiness to loved ones, guiding them towards a happier life, like showing your children the way.
- You can fully appreciate and maximize the happiness from what you already possess.
- You can eliminate suffering within your own mind.
- You can live a successful and contented life with the added energy and positivity from being happy.
- You can get happiness under your control.
- You can be the author of your happy life.

Simply by reading this book, you are on your way to greater happiness!

MY HAPPINESS JOURNEY

I was born in Sri Lanka, a beautiful island in the Indian Ocean. In 1999 I graduated from the University of Moratuwa with a degree in computer science and engineering. I then traveled to Poughkeepsie,

New York, to join IBM as an intern. Leaving Sri Lanka for the first time to move to New York was a significant event in my life, and I was beyond excited.

When I completed my internship, I left IBM and went on a journey to work and explore the world. Soon I was building systems for organizations the United Kingdom, Canada, Saudi Arabia, and the UAE. I married a beautiful girl from Sri Lanka, and we finally settled in Vancouver, Canada, bought a big house to live in and had two beautiful children. Life was good, and I was expecting to live happily ever after.

Then came the financial crisis of 2008. Like most, the company I worked at began cost-cutting measures right and left and started focusing only on profit. The people around me were unhappy. I was neck-deep in the rat race before I knew what was happening. I was miserable at work, which soon carried over into my home life.

I was unhappy with my marriage. My wife and I had different expectations for ourselves and each other. On our days off I would spend time out of the house engaging in fun activities while my wife would stay home and rest after a busy week. These expectations created rifts in my marriage. Little things began to add up, eventually the little things became big things and after a few years, we separated.

Our kids were four and five years old when we started going through a tough divorce. During this time, anger began to creep in. My mind was cluttered, and I was failing miserably at life. On the outside we looked successful, working for a leading bank with a happy home and happy family, but on the inside we were frustrated, upset and falling apart.

The trauma I developed from the divorce revealed many internal scars I had carried from childhood. Thoughts of *I am not good enough, nobody loves me, I do not belong* constantly ran through my mind. I had been programmed with those self-limiting beliefs ever since I was young. I grew up in a middle-income household with my dad, an insurance advisor, and my mother, a teacher. They enrolled me in a famous school in Sri Lanka. My elementary school teacher doubted my eligibility for enrolment, since the school was out of my catchment area, and he asked me how I could have possibly been able to attend that school. I was nine years old, and I started to think that I was not good enough, that I didn't belong, and nobody loved me. Those old programs lingered in my head throughout my life and surfaced during the divorce, hurting me again.

I tried different things to be successful once more. I enrolled in financial education programs, but without a clear mind I could not do well in them. Then I started another relationship, thinking that would solve the problem. We both had unresolved issues from our childhoods. Although we had great times, we also engaged in terrible fights, which ended up in me getting kicked out of the house. I couldn't fight back, nor did I want to. I had a backpack, a few clothes, a passport, and a laptop. Driving down the highway I felt completely alone and lost, with no family or a place to call home, and I didn't even know where I was going. I felt like I had lost everything. I eventually pulled over and checked into a hotel. Unable to figure out what had happened to my life and not knowing what to do, I called a friend, moved into their basement, and tried to figure my life out.

A few days later I decided to go to the office and talk to my manager. He was a nice, calm guy, so I sat down with him and explained that I needed to leave to go discover the meaning of life.

He shared with me about how he had once taken a break to discover different aspects of life when he was young. He gave me his blessings, and I left my job.

I took the opportunity to return to Sri Lanka and attend a spiritual retreat. I meditated for nine days straight. During that time, I let go of all the clutter in my head. Little by little, I started to see life more clearly. I did many things to understand myself and life. I participated in personal-development workshops and meditation and energy-healing programs, read many books, found mentors, and did a lot of spiritual activities. And finally, I saw something unique. I realized all unhappiness starts from negative thoughts, and I saw how to end the suffering of the mind. I understood each negative thought on a deeper level and ultimately defeated them.

I did not stop there. That's when I truly started my happiness journey. I discovered how to overcome all my problems and create sustainable happiness. After many years of extensive research and practice, I reached the top of Happiness Mountain. I discovered what true happiness means.

THE HAPPINESS DEFINITION

Life is a journey of experiences, and happiness is the result of six specific experiences:

- **Happiness Experience One:** Living with full positive energy using Positive Power-Ups
- **Happiness Experience Two:** Living without stress or worry by stopping negative Thought Bugs
- **Happiness Experience Three:** Living a joyful and balanced life using four Happy Hormones
- **Happiness Experience Four:** Living with inner happiness by connecting to your Higher Self
- **Happiness Experience Five:** Living your greatness through giving back
- **Happiness Experience Six:** Life fulfillment with happiness, health, wealth, and doing what you love

You can enjoy a **mountain of happiness** by consciously creating all **six happiness experiences**. The Happiness Mountain methodology in this book describes how you can acquire each happiness experience through self-awareness.

VALIDATION OF THE HAPPINESS DEFINITION

At the beginning of this chapter, I noted no clear definition of happiness (until Happiness Mountain declared one). A friend of mine posed an insightful question. Could it be because the expectation of happiness varies from person to person? On the surface of it, expectations are different. On the other hand, all human beings experience happiness from these six experiences, whether they are aware of it or not:

- Happiness Experience One: Living with full positive energy
- Happiness Experience Two: Living without stress or worry
- Happiness Experience Three: Living a joyful and balanced life using four Happy Hormones
- Happiness Experience Four: Living with inner happiness by connecting to your Higher Self
- Happiness Experience Five: Living your greatness through giving back
- Happiness Experience Six: Life fulfillment with happiness, health, wealth, and doing what you love

The above six experiences cause your happiness, and various expectations and activities are pathways to these experiences. For instance, when you meet a friend and share a bond, love and trust, your body releases the 'oxytocin' happy hormone, creating a wonderful feeling, as highlighted in 'Happiness Experience Three.' While you and I may have different friends, the underlying factor driving happiness remains consistent - Joy from happy hormones.

Various teachings exist about life and happiness. Some emphasize joy, others focus on achieving goals, while some delve into spirituality or promote positivity. At 'Happiness Mountain', all these teachings converge. Once you ascend Happiness Mountain, you gain a comprehensive understanding. Engaging with other teachings thereafter will provide you with even clearer insights, enriched by your journey up the mountain.

HAPPINESS FOUNDATION:

Staying positive, eliminating worries and stress, and cultivating joy are the cornerstones of happiness. This is where I recommend everyone begin.

- Happiness Experience One: True happiness arises when you maintain a positive outlook. The moment negativity creeps in, happiness slips away.
- Happiness Experience Two: Even with abundant material possessions and favorable circumstances, happiness eludes you if you are burdened with worries or stress.
- Happiness Experience Three: Experiencing joy is fundamental to happiness. Sometimes, people think joy is the happiness. It is a crucial part of happiness, and there are five more experiences to the completeness of happiness.

ADVANCED:

Let's delve into the advanced aspects of happiness.

- Happiness Experience Four: Inner happiness and peace of mind are paramount for your happiness. Without Inner Happiness, your happiness remains superficial. For genuine, inside-out happiness, inner contentment and peace are vital.
- Happiness Experience Five: A purpose-driven life elevates your happiness. Without recognizing greatness in you, life may seem empty, preventing your happiness from reaching its peak.

PINNACLE:

To experience the pinnacle of happiness, consider the following together with foundation and advanced elements.

Happiness Experience Six: To attain peak happiness, one must find fulfillment in various life dimensions—health, wealth, relationships, and more. Without such fulfillment, there might always be a lingering feeling of something missing, hindering your journey to the peak of happiness. On the other hand, when you are on the top of the mountain, you can enjoy good fortune and prosperity with all the energy that you accumulated by being truly happy.

HOW TO EXPERIENCE A MOUNTAIN OF HAPPINESS

Every experience is fundamental in your quest for happiness. In the next chapter, "**Happiness Methodology**," you'll be introduced to **how** to unlock each of these experiences. My ambition is to present knowledge in a way that, no matter your current situation, you'll find the path to a truly happy life. With "Happiness Mountain," I simplify the journey to ultimate happiness. The essence is awareness, and this book is your guide, equipping you with the clarity, tools, and techniques to effortlessly climb the Happiness Mountain.

Not knowing happiness, I spent my years of life with unhappiness. Now, I live a phenomenally happy life on the top of Happiness Mountain. And many people who climbed it do the same. People who read the book claim it is a well-structured methodology to gain true happiness.

> I keep practicing the Happy Mountain book and reading all the chapters. I can't believe I was ever happy as now. My mind is more relaxed, and I see things clearly. I keep finding happiness in each simple experience. Also, some days are challenging, but I now know how to overcome them and find joy and happi-

ness. I am grateful to Happiness Mountain for showing me the true happiness.

— ARUNI UDAYANTHI, FEDERAL PUBLIC SERVANT

> Happiness Mountain is a clever, simple yet brilliant book to guide you on your path to happiness. With love flowing through on every page, this book has clearly been written with heart, integrity and compassion, you won't be able to stop reading. I highly recommend this book to everyone who is looking for happiness and fulfillment!

— TARA BROCKWAY, ADMINISTRATIVE ASSISTANT

> I believe everyone, irrespective of their religion or belief, can try this book's techniques for achieving ultimate happiness.

— SUDARSHAN MAITHRE, ACCOUNTING PROFESSIONAL

> It's absolutely possible to have more joy and happiness in your life. Happiness Mountain book has really laid out a practical method to do this in a very thoughtful, easy to follow way.

— JACK CANFIELD, NEW YORK TIMES BESTSELLING AUTHOR OF THE 'CHICKEN SOUP FOR THE SOUL' SERIES & 'THE SUCCESS PRINCIPLES'

APPLICATION TO DAILY LIFE

Here's a simple daily affirmation based on the definition of happiness::

- I make every experience a happy experience
- I live with full positive energy
- I live without stress and worries
- I live a joyful and balanced life
- I live with inner happiness
- I release my greatness
- I enjoy a fulfilled life with happiness, health, wealth, and doing what you love

You can download the affirmation worksheet from: happiness-mountain.com/book/resources.

Or you can use The Happiness Mountain App which is coming soon to the App Store and Google Play Store. Stay updated by registering for our newsletter at www.happinessmountain.com.

Now that you understand what true happiness entails, let's explore the 'Happiness Methodology' in the next chapter.

CHAPTER 2
HAPPINESS METHODOLOGY

Happiness Mountain methodology shows you how you can, step by step, unlock the six happiness experiences in the happiness definition that you learned in the previous chapter.

Happiness Mountain

HAPPINESS MOUNTAIN

There are many mountains in the world. When climbing one, you need to start from the bottom. You cannot jump to the middle or the top just because you have climbed other mountains. You may climb faster or more efficiently if you are experienced, but you must always start from the bottom.

The same principle applies to climbing Happiness Mountain. When embarking on this adventure, I advise you to start from the beginning. I have seen many people struggling to find inner peace and life fulfillment because they have not learned to stop negative energy. Starting from the bottom is crucial for everyone, even if you believe you have lifted your mind to higher levels.

LIVING WITH FULL POSITIVE ENERGY

Happiness Experience One

Suppose you buy an electric car. If you do not charge it daily, you cannot use it. If you charge it only a little bit, it may not have enough power and run out of energy in the middle of the day. If you fully charge the car, you can drive without running out of energy. Similarly, you need a daily full charge of positive energy to feel great from when you wake up till you go to bed. You are a unique and great human being. Without charging, you cannot get your full power.

Let us look at how you can charge yourself with energy. Human beings come with extraordinary traits. The way to charge yourself is to use the great human traits you were born with. I call the following traits **Positive Power-Ups:**

- Gratitude Power-Up
- Uplift Power-Up
- Love Power-Up
- Acceptance Power-Up
- Patience Power-Up
- Moderation Power-Up
- Mindfulness Power-Up

- Integrity Power-Up

There are many positive traits, but the eight above are carefully selected for happiness. You probably know these traits as words, but you may not use them with intention. Let's take *love* as an example. What is love? Happiness Mountain has a precise meaning for it that will help you implement it in life: a package consisting of blessings, empathy, compassion, acts of kindness, and forgiveness. Say you become upset with your loved one. You can use the love package to radiate true love.

You require Power-Ups to overcome the negative energy that is generated by you and others. Having a set of well-understood Power-Ups is crucial to living a happy life. You will learn clear definitions for all the Power-Ups, with examples on how to apply them in the Happiness Experience One section of this book. You will learn how to make them your core values and establish a resilient mind.

LIVING WITHOUT STRESS OR WORRY

Happiness Experience Two

We love to create a comfortable life for ourselves and our loved ones. Let's say you want to fill a bucket with water. (In life, you would fill it with things like happiness, health, and wealth.) If you have a leaky bucket, you can try to fill it but it will never be full. The first thing you must do is patch the holes.

In life, even if you know how to create positive energy, you cannot fully charge yourself if there are energy leaks. These holes are the harmful thoughts creating negative energy. Happiness Mountain defines eight negative thoughts that take away your happiness. For sustainable happiness, you must understand and overcome them. On Happiness Mountain, we call them **Thought Bugs**:

- Anger Thought Bug
- Worry Thought Bug

- Expectation Thought Bug
- Craving Thought Bug
- Judgment Thought Bug
- Fear Thought Bug
- Self-Limiting Thought Bug
- Do-it-Later Thought Bug

Awareness of these negative Thought Bugs and knowing how to eliminate them is crucial for your happiness. Once you climb level two, you will see a beautiful view of your life without the impact of negative thoughts. You will not let negative thoughts creep into your everyday actions. Imagine your life full of happiness when you take care of the above negative thoughts.

You are going to learn about each negative Thought Bug in the Happiness Experience Two section of this book.

LIVING A JOYFUL AND BALANCED LIFE

HAPPINESS EXPERIENCE THREE

What do you do from the time you wake up until you go to bed? My patterns before climbing Happiness Mountain were taking care of family responsibilities and work responsibilities during weekdays. At nighttime, if I had time, I would watch movies on video-on-demand platforms. On the weekend, I would plan activities such as going out with friends.

Now I have changed that mindset to see life as a series of experiences. From the time I wake up till I go to bed, I see my life a collection of experiences, and I have learned to make every experience joyful. For example, if I make breakfast for my kids, I consider it an *experience*. I do it with love and serve breakfast at my best.

Think about going on a holiday and staying in a nice hotel. You go to breakfast, and the server serves you a nice meal. You feel good. At home, making a meal and serving it to the family is a great experience you can have daily. I change my mindset from "doing a task" to "performing an enjoyable experience." How do you get the joy out of every experience that appears to be work or a series of tasks? Happy Hormones are the secret to making work or tasks enjoyable experiences. You can consciously trigger Happy Hormones in every experience.

In biological terms, there are only four Happy Hormones. I remember them as DOSE (**D**opamine, **O**xytocin, **S**erotonin, and **E**ndorphins). The key benefit they offer is making my experiences joyful. Each **DOSE** hormone has unique features:

1. **D**opamine: drive, motivation, and pleasure
2. **O**xytocin: bonding, trust, and love
3. **S**erotonin: elevated mood and self-esteem
4. **E**ndorphins: healing and well-being

Don't you want joy in everything you do? Most people think you have to do different activities to trigger Happy Hormones. Happiness Mountain methodology uses Happy Hormones like they are salt and pepper to make *every* experience enjoyable. With knowledge of Happy Hormones, you can gain *conscious* happiness instead of waiting for *accidental* happiness to occur.

Let's look at an example to understand conscious happiness. You meet a friend, which makes you feel good after. You meet another friend and do not feel good; instead, you think negatively. With the first friend, you felt love, a bond, and trust, and the body triggered oxytocin so that you became happy. You did not have love, a bond, or trust with the other friend, so your body did not trigger oxytocin, and you did not feel joy. Awareness is your power. With it, you can do one of two things: you fix the love, bond, and trust with the second friend by making an authentic connection, or you can decide to not waste your time with them. I use Happy Hormones' knowledge extensively to make every experience a happy one.

You are going to learn about DOSE in detail, and how to apply them in daily life in the Happiness Experience Three section of this book.

LIVING WITH INNER HAPPINESS

Happiness Experience Four

In life, we get a lot of education. For example, I earned a bachelor's degree in computer science and engineering. On top of that, I did many certifications related to my career. I did everything to create a promising career and live a happy life. Yet I did not learn enough about happiness. At the end of the day, the human mind is what makes us happy. When I realized that, I started studying the human mind and how it relates to our happiness. Then a question came to me: Who am I? Ask yourself that question. Who are you?

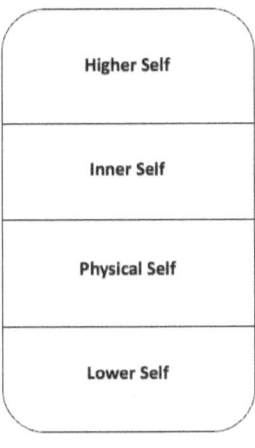

You are a creation with four dimensions

To gain inner happiness, you have to understand *you*. Happiness Mountain defines you as a creation consisting of four dimensions - Inner Self, Physical Self, Lower Self, and Higher Self.

People often drive their life from three dimensions: their Inner Self, Physical Self, and Lower Self. When you learn to guide your life from your Higher Self, it is easy to find inner peace. Happiness Mountain has the methodology to activate and connect to your Higher Self. The world is going through a lot of challenges, such as pandemics, wars, economic downturns, and division among people. Energy from these negative situations can impact your inner happiness unless you have a resilient mind. Your Higher Self will make your mind resilient. The sooner you activate your Higher Self, the sooner you can navigate the challenging world with inner peace.

You are going to learn how to activate your Higher Self in the Happiness Experience Four section of this book.

FIND YOUR GREATNESS

HAPPINESS EXPERIENCE FIVE

The path to greatness is in giving back. Greatness entitles you to have:
- Happiness
- Health
- Wealth
- Respect
- Self-esteem
- Life fulfillment
- Abundance

Do you know that there are nine types of ways to give back? In Happiness Mountain, you are going to learn all nine give-backs to discover your greatness. Awareness is your power. Happiness Mountain gives you the awareness to empower you to discover your greatness. By giving back, you can create an inspiring life for yourself and others.

You are going to learn all nine give-backs in the Happiness Experience Five section of this book.

LIFE FULFILLMENT

HAPPINESS EXPERIENCE SIX

Welcome to the top of Happiness Mountain, where it's about your life fulfillment. I wanted to live a fulfilled life, and I am sure you do too. Then I thought, *What life fulfillment?* I encountered the same problem of not knowing why, how, or what. Without a clear view of your life fulfillment, you could end up working hard and not being fulfilled.

Happiness Mountain has a **Life Fulfillment Map** to help you with that.

Domains	Intentions
Mind	Happy and peaceful mind
Body	Healthy active body
Personal interests	Do what you love
Family	Loving and caring family
Work	Serve others while enjoying work-life happiness
Social	A good relationship with friends, mentors, and community
Wealth	A satisfactory amount of wealth
Giveback	Make positive impacts by giving back
Optional	
Romance	Love and intimacy with your partner
Business	Business to serve the world and create more wealth

Life fulfillment map

You will learn to take advantage of the law of vibration, the law of creation, and the law of attraction to attain fulfillment. It would be best if you focused on your fulfillment and do not try to be perfect or do what others want you to do. You are the author of your life. Happiness Mountain's Life Fulfillment Map has ten domains, and each fulfills you in its own way.

You are going to learn how to fulfill your life in the Happiness Experience Six section of this book.

You can climb Happiness Mountain at your own pace. If you stay in experience one or experience two, you are still going to achieve happiness. When you are ready, you can decide to go to the next level, the next experience. No matter where you are, you are on your journey on Happiness Mountain. What matters most is the fact that you are on it.

Why is a methodology critical? A methodology can be followed by anyone, and they will gain results. You do not have to reinvent a methodology for happiness. Instead, follow the Happiness Mountain methodology with ease. You can customize it the way it best suits you.

Irrespective of where you are in life today, by reading this book and following the happiness methodology, you or anyone can live a happier life.

To achieve success in any journey, a guiding philosophy is essential. In the next chapter, I'll share the Happiness Philosophy that will help make you truly happier every single day.

CHAPTER 3
HAPPINESS PHILOSOPHY

 Make Every Experience a Happy Experience

— AMAL INDI

Every day, from the time you wake up to when you sleep, is a collection of experiences. By changing the philosophy of happiness to *make every experience a happy experience,* you can genuinely live a happier life. If you make every experience happy, naturally, your whole day will be happy. If you focus on happiness daily, your entire life will be happy. You do not need to wait for something to happen or some future activity to be happy. Instead, cultivate happiness here and now, in the present moment, and in every experience.

To live in this new happiness philosophy "make every experience a happy experience," you need to be aware of yourself and have the right skills. Learning about Happiness Mountain's way of seeing happiness and the approach will help you get those skills and insights.

DAILY EXPERIENCES

Let's get more clarity on your experiences. During the day, you go through ten to twenty experiences based on how you look at your daily life. Here's a glimpse into a typical day in my life experiences breakdown:

1. Morning Ritual: I wake up and engage in my morning routine, rejuvenating my energy and setting the tone for the day ahead.
2. Writing Session: I dedicate an hour each morning to writing as an author.
3. Morning Walk: I go for a walk and sometimes get my coffee from my favorite coffee shop.
4. Family Time: I assist my children with breakfast and help them prepare for school.
5. Work: Depending on the missions, this could be divided into five or six separate experiences.
6. Evening Tasks: I prepare dinner for my children after work.
7. Household Activities: This includes tidying up and cleaning the house.
8. Relaxation: I indulge in some leisure time, which might involve browsing social media, watching videos, or chatting with loved ones. If needed, I'll also assist my children with their homework.
9. Physical Fitness: I visit the gym, attend a cardio class, or participate in a yoga session.
10. Night Routine: I wind down, prepare for bed, and reflect on the day's events.

Take a moment to think about your regular days and the experiences you have.

HAPPINESS MOUNTAIN'S APPROACH

In each of above experiences, I consciously apply the philosophy of Happiness Mountain. By merely setting the intention to find happiness in every experience, our minds intuitively discover avenues to enhance our happiness.

Then, I apply the Happiness Definition.

- I make every experience positive.
- I make every experience worry and stress-free
- I make every experience joyful
- I make every experience peaceful with my higher self
- I radiate my greatness in every experience
- I seek fulfillment in each experience

Another distinction I want to make in the Happiness Philosophy is that you convert tasks to experiences. For instance, before discovering Happiness Mountain, preparing dinner for my children felt like just another chore. Now, it's an experience I love – an act of service to my family, done with love and mindfulness. It's become an opportunity to express my gratitude to them, making it a fulfilling and rewarding part of my day.

Of course, not every experience is without its challenges. Should a hurdle arise, I turn to the strategies of Happiness Mountain's methodology. If someone attempts to steer an experience in a negative direction, I first shield my mind using the Positive Power-Ups, like employing Acceptance Power-Up. I remain vigilant against letting others' negativity trigger my "Thought Bugs." Instead, I connect with my higher self, seeking solutions to enhance the situation. If it doesn't seem immediately resolvable, I practice Patience Power-Up, letting time and healing run their course. As you can see, my happiness isn't by chance but rather by awareness, guided by Happiness Mountain.

THE POWER OF THE MIND, LIKE A GPS

Our minds are powerful. Think of it like a GPS. When you tell yourself, "I want to make this experience a happy experience," your mind will show you the way. It's like giving directions to your GPS. Suddenly, you'll have bright ideas pop up. Grab those ideas quickly and do something about them. If you wait too long, the feeling and energy might go away. There are things that can stop you, like waiting too long (that's the Do-it-Later Bug) or not believing in yourself (that's the Self-Limiting Bug). But now you know how your mind-GPS works, so you can overcome those Thought Bugs and use the power of the mind to create a happier you.

Throughout this book, these principles and techniques will become more apparent. This chapter introduces the philosophy of Happiness Mountain and illustrates its profound impact on everyday life.

CHAPTER 4
FOUR QUADRANTS OF HAPPINESS

Spiritual Happiness	Phenomenal Happiness
Inner Happiness	Temporary Happiness

Four Quadrants of Happiness

When you climb Happiness Mountain, you come across four types of happiness. These four quadrants contain different types of energies. In life, you may have experienced these energies without awareness. When you have the understanding, you can design your life as needed. You can be the author of your life filled with different types of energies. All four types are great, and you can experience all of them in life.

INNER HAPPINESS

When you have Inner Happiness, you are positive, worry, and stress-free and find peace in life. You can unlock your Inner Happiness by

- **Happiness Experience One:** Living with full positive energy using Positive Power-Ups
- **Happiness Experience Two:** Living without stress or worry by stopping negative Thought Bugs
- **Happiness Experience Four:** Living with inner happiness by connecting to your Higher Self

Happiness Experiences One and Two give you intermittent peace, and Happiness Experience Four will provide your sustainable Inner Happiness with resiliency.

In this quadrant, you have more peaceful energy.

TEMPORARY HAPPINESS

Temporary Happiness is all about joy arising from four Happy Hormones. Hormones are momentary and your Temporary Happiness as well. You are enjoying Temporary Happiness by

Happiness Experience Three: Living a joyful and balanced life using four Happy Hormones

In this quadrant, you have more joyful energy. If you experience too much joy without balance, you can quickly lose the joy and go to worries and stress. Joy in balance and mixed with other happiness types is the best experience. Consider joy as the salt for a meal. It would help to have it for an overall happiness meal but don't put it too much.

SPIRITUAL HAPPINESS

When you are in Spiritual Happiness, you are more connected to your Higher Self and less attached to the material things. You can discover more of your Spiritual Happiness by

- **Happiness Experience Four:** Living with inner happiness by connecting to your Higher Self
- **Happiness Experience Five:** Living your greatness through giving back

In this quadrant, you will have peace and harmony within. You learn to become happier from the inside, and because of less strong attachments and giving back, you will feel great within.

PHENOMENAL HAPPINESS

Phenomenal Happiness is about life fulfillment and success. You can create the life you love: happiness, fulfillment, and success. You have the choice. Enjoys material things without attachment and has peace, wealth, health, and joy in life. You will feel this when you are on the top of the Happiness Mountain.

Happiness Experience Six: Life fulfillment with happiness, health, wealth, and doing what you love

In this quadrant, you will feel the fulfillment and success energy with all other energies - peace, joy, and harmony in balance.

CHAPTER 5
REPROGRAMMING YOUR MIND FOR HAPPINESS

Visualize a ship going to different destinations in the sea. Sometimes the ship gets anchored. After doing necessary maintenance and restocking what's required for the journey, remove the anchor and sail to another destination. The sea is your life journey, and the ship is your life. The sea is beautiful, and at times it gets rough with storms. A well-maintained vessel can withstand those turbulent times and move to a calm, beautiful sea again. If the ship stays anchored for many years and you don't take care of it, it can get rusty and not fit to sail.

If you are reading this book, you are not anchored. You know the enjoyment of sailing and taking care of your vessel, your mind and body. You are now upgrading your ship by reprogramming your mind to be happier. To reprogram, start understanding your mind and the old damaging programs running within you. Those damaging programs are getting your ship rusty without you seeing them. You gained some destructive programs without your knowledge while growing up, but they can be reprogrammed. Once you reprogram old unwanted programs, you get a happier mind. With a happier mind you can have great relationships and financial stability, help others, and live a fulfilled life.

Happiness Mountain's philosophy is to improve yourself throughout your life journey. It is never late for anyone to climb Happiness Mountain, remove the anchor, and start moving up to a higher vibe. You have one life, and you should be the best version of yourself. Make an impact in the world. Feel good in your mind and body. When you do, you feel good about everything else in life. You become happy inside and out.

PERSONAS

While discussing certain concepts, I am taking stories from my life. I like to introduce my two personas when talking about how I discovered reprogramming.

Persona One: Yasantha

Yasantha is my childhood persona, where I was programmed into young adulthood from the circumstances of my upbringing. I had little control over them.

- **Mind**: Negative thoughts and survival were the drivers of the mind, with temporary happiness activities to compensate for the hard work.
- **Body**: Mind-body not in harmony and unaware of how to use Happy Hormones.
- **Energy**: Unbalanced by responsibilities, desires, stress, and worries. Energy is wasted to run in the rat race.

Persona Two: Amal

Amal is the persona I created with a conscious mind to thrive, to break all the self-imposed limitations in me. I consciously programmed my mind to be happy and fulfilled using the Happiness Mountain methodology.

Below you can see a few of the distinctions between the two personas.

- **Mind**: Clean positive thoughts based on Happiness Mountain. Happiness and fulfillment are the drivers of the mind. Focus is making every experience a happy experience.
- **Body**: Mind-body connected and in harmony. Use Happy Hormones to create joyful and balanced life.
- **Energy**: Knows how to overcome negative energy effectively without living in stress or worries. Have surplus positive energy to make a positive impact in the world.

EVERYONE CAN CHANGE THEIR PERSONA

Let's see how to determine your different personas. Think of it as if you are in a drama: You use different personas. You are already doing that. How you engage at home vs. your workplace is different. Am I correct? When you go out with your friends, you use a different persona. When you are with kids, you act differently. You are born with this ability. You may not have the consciousness of these personas, but you can reprogram them as you wish. Our focus on Happiness Mountain is reprogramming a persona to live a happy and fulfilling life. The new you become consciously happy instead of accidentally happy.

BODY MEMORY

Body Memory is a concept that you can use during reprogramming. Your past experiences and how you felt are stored in your body memory. When you are reprogramming, it is vital to create happy experiences so that your memory contains good experiences that your mind and body want to repeat again and again. Body memory is like a lake containing all your memories. If you have happy experiences, the memory lake in your body becomes clean and beautiful.

Clean Lake   Polluted Lake

Clean Memory vs Polluted Memory

- **Question One:** What makes your body memory polluted? The answer is Negative Thought Bugs.
- **Question Two**: How to keep body memory clean? The answer is by using Positive Power-Ups.

In the next two parts of the book, you are going to learn Positive Power-Ups and Negative Thought Bugs. Let's start filling your memory lake with consciously created happy experiences using Happiness Mountain. Add one happy experience at a time. Eventually, you will have a beautiful memory lake filled with great experiences.

Happiness Experience One: Living with Full Positive Energy

CHAPTER 6
EIGHT POSITIVE POWER-UPS: KEYS TO POSITIVE ENERGY

You have heard the phrase "be a good human." You might wonder why you want to be one, and how you can become one. What makes a human good? In the happiness context, if you live with positive energy, you are a good human being. You must follow the human traits that are fundamental to happiness to truly become happy. You will worry if you do not follow good human traits. You could be acquiring material things, but you will never live in peace.

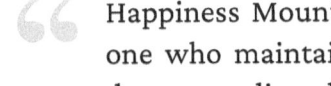

> Happiness Mountain's definition of a good human is one who maintains a surplus of positive energy and does not radiate dark energies to the world.
>
> —AMAL INDI

To be a good human being and enjoy Happiness Experience One: Living with full positive energy, you must learn how to generate, protect, and maintain your positive energy.

I believe you have learned many good traits from your childhood and are still learning. As I got older, I realized I was learning more and more and not consciously practicing traits that I had already learned. Positive-thinking quotes make you feel good for only a few seconds. I decided to focus on a few human traits and be good at them. I wanted to practice the ones that give me happiness and peace of mind. The question is, which ones? I tested many and defined **eight Positive Power-Ups** to be the most fundamental traits. I implemented them from the bottom of my heart as my core values.

Now I am a happiness millionaire. I stay in my Higher Self using Positive Power-Ups and solve every challenge in life without suffering from worries, anger, judgments, etc. Positive Power-Ups are the shortest path to your peace of mind. Let's understand what, why, and how to implement them in your life.

POSITIVE POWER-UPS

There are three Positive Power-Up categories based on how they help to generate, stabilize, and protect your energy.

Energy amplifiers:
Gratitude
Uplift

Energy protectors:
Love
Acceptance
Patience
Moderation

Energy stabilizers:
Mindfulness
Integrity

Whenever you lose peace of mind, you can see which Positive Power-Up can help you bring it back. I was able to overcome all my life's struggles by implementing these eight traits. They are magical and powerful. Focus on getting good at them all.

Power-ups in video games give you more energy and protect you from enemies. It is the same concept here. These eight Positive Power-Ups will provide you with more energy and protect you from negative energy.

DO YOU NEED POSITIVE POWER-UPS?

- Do you want to have peace of mind?
- Do you want to protect yourself from negative people?
- Do you want to live a fulfilling life?
- Do you want to have a happy daily life?

If you said yes to any of the above, your easiest path to achieve them is by implementing Positive Power-Ups as core values. You might wonder what "core values" are. They are the fundamental beliefs that drive your behaviors, how you live your life. For example, when you are upset with someone, you have guiding principles to resolve the issue if you have core values. You are always at peace. Positive Power-Ups are the perfect set of core values you can live for the rest of your life.

HOW TO USE POSITIVE POWER-UPS

I knew the word *acceptance*, but I did not power my life up with it. Not knowing how to power up acceptance caused:

- Family issues and unhappiness, and a divorce
- Dissatisfaction with friends
- Unhappiness at work
- Unhappy community engagements

That is how I caused my suffering. From the outside, everything looked good with my life. I had a job, family, friends, and community engagements. Before I found Happiness Mountain, I suffered due to a lack of applying good human traits to my life.

After consciously applying Positive Power-Ups, I realized how easy life is. I first needed to learn the true meaning of each Power-Up and how to apply them in real life, which you will learn in the next few chapters.

CREATE A SURPLUS OF POSITIVE ENERGY

Your net energy could be negative, positive, or neutral on a given day. You feel truly positive when you have surplus of positive energy.

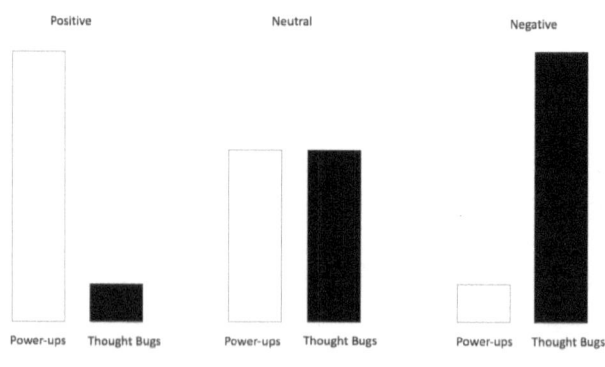

Focus on your net energy

Your daily happiness reflects your net energy. Surplus positive energy is fundamental to your happiness. To live a happy life, you must first elevate your energy and help others boost theirs.

WHY POSITIVE ENERGY IS IMPORTANT

Weeds vs Flowers

- **Weeds in mind** = negative energy from the use of Negative Thought Bugs
- **Flowers in mind** = positive energy from the use of Positive Power-ups

Your mind is like a garden. If you do not care for it, weeds will grow. Maintain your mind like a beautiful garden, then your whole day becomes peaceful and happy. You have more energy to do things better. Your attitude becomes great. Your health becomes better. You become beautiful inside and out.

In the following few chapters, you will learn what each of the Positive Power-Ups means and how to reprogram them into your core value system.

CHAPTER 7
GRATITUDE POWER-UP

Life is a gift. Give gratitude to open it.

WHAT IS GRATITUDE?

We all have goals and desires in life. We also have responsibilities. We tend to get busy quickly with our responsibilities and goals. We start thinking about the day ahead and into the future. We want to create a secure future in an impermanent life. Busy life makes us forget the blessings that we have right now. When you look at people struggling in the world with poverty, war, and many other afflictions, you will realize how blessed you are. Yet do you have time to give gratitude to what you have, stay in peace, and reflect on how much you are blessed with? Are you still complaining about things happening in your life?

Gratitude means taking a pause, looking around at your present situation, and being appreciative of it all. It is also important to give gratitude to the people who have helped you come this far. It could be anyone: parents, teachers, former partners, mentors, etc.

WHY GRATITUDE IS IMPORTANT

Your life is a gift. Are you enjoying it? There is only one way to open the gift: by being grateful. If you can see the blessings in your life every day, you have opened the life gift. Some people are so busy that they do not have time to open the gift. Some worry so much about life that they do not recognize the gift of *right now*, the present moment, but rather they remain in the rat race, always seeking something better. Every single day is a gift for you to be happy and to make a positive impact on your life and others. Life will not last forever. Open the gift with gratitude every morning. Then make every experience a happy one. Your life is happening today. If you refuse to show gratitude, you are missing your life.

HOW TO LIVE WITH GRATITUDE

Now, look around. What do you see? I see myself alive. I see my home. I see my children. I see beautiful trees outside the window. Give gratitude to your life, home, family, and Mother Nature. If you count your blessings right now you will see that there are many, but the mind always looks for what is not there—for example, a broken relationship or financial difficulty. Recognize that the nature of your mind is to look for what you do not have. When you appreciate what you have and give gratitude, you will suddenly see heaven on earth in front of you.

It is not only what you own legally. You can thank the parks, malls, gyms, restaurants, and everything you consume. It is incredible how many things are available for you to enjoy. You just have to actually see them. Did you ever think that the park you go to for a walk is yours? You are consuming it by enjoying it. It is a gift from the universe to you. The city is maintaining it for you. How lucky you are to have that park in the neighborhood.

I am the wealthiest person in the world because I consider everything I consume to be mine. I enjoy many parks, mountains, shopping malls, and beaches, and I do not even have to maintain them. I do not limit what is mine only to what I own. You came to the world empty and you will leave empty. You cannot take anything with you when you die. Legally owning something means you have extra maintenance responsibilities. It is even better if you can enjoy the experiences without owning them. I pay taxes, of course. Indirectly I am paying for most of the amazing things the city owns. I make sure I take time to enjoy them. And they are mine to experience in this life. Now it is your turn to own as many properties as you like. Go to a park or beach and claim your virtual ownership by experiencing it with lots of Happy Hormones. Give gratitude to the city and everyone who maintains it. If you can, go around the world and own as many things as you can by experiencing them.

I want to add one more thing about the expensive housing market: Do not worry too much about legal ownership if you do not have your dream home yet. Work on it while virtually having a lot of properties. Your dream home is your city, country, and world. If you have the time and mindset to enjoy everything available, you are wealthier than you think.

WHEN TO GIVE GRATITUDE

There are four powerful gratitude-giving moments:

- In the morning
- Before going to bed
- Before eating
- At the start of every experience

IN THE MORNING

I do gratitude journaling every morning using the Happiness Mountain app. If you are not an app user, keep a journal. I start by writing, "I am grateful for my life." I give gratitude for everything that comes to my mind at that moment. Writing it will make it more tangible than thinking it. Here are some examples of what you can give gratitude to:

- People you live with (parents, spouse, kids)
- The home you live in
- The city you live in
- The country you live in
- Your job
- The people you work with by name, individually
- People you met today or yesterday
- Your teachers, mentors, and coaches
- People you have conflicts or frictions with (see their good side)
- Your former partners, if any (think about the good times you had)
- Your things, such as a house, bed, cars, properties, and money

As you can see, once you open the gratitude gate your mind will see a new dimension of the life you are already living. I cannot fully describe gratitude happiness in words. You must experience it. Once you enjoy the taste of joy created by giving gratitude, you will always do it. Until you open the gratitude gate in your mind, you need to put in the effort. Trust me, it is worth it.

BEFORE GOING TO BED

Do you want to have a good sleep? Giving gratitude is a great way to end your day and go to bed for an excellent happy sleep. There is another powerful benefit of doing it just before bed. When you give gratitude before bed it goes to your subconscious mind, a part of your mind that makes decisions without needing to actively put effort into it. It is like an autopilot mode of you. If you give gratitude and become happy before bed, your subconscious mind registers that you are happy and grateful for your life. Then you make decisions that make you happy and grateful even without actively needing to think about them. Your next day becomes happy and grateful without even having to think about it, because it comes from your subconscious mind. Offer gratitude consistently and make it a habit.

WHILE EATING

In my family, we always offer gratitude before eating:

- To the person who made the food
- To the people who helped prepare the food
- If ordered through food delivery service, to the person who brought food to us
- For having food on the table

DURING EVERY EXPERIENCE

Happiness Mountain's philosophy is to make every experience a happy one. One of the critical elements to this is giving gratitude at the beginning of every experience. During the day you could experience ten to thirty or more experiences, depending on how you see them. For example, when I get in the car and drive, I take that as one experience. I am grateful to have a car. When I go to work, I give gratitude to coworkers and the company. When I start a business meeting, I give gratitude to the people who join the meeting. When I go to the gym, I give gratitude to the staff and everyone who is helping to maintain the gym. Throughout the day, give gratitude for every different experience and make it a habit. Giving gratitude is a superpower you possess. Use it to make every day a happy day.

CHAPTER 8
UPLIFT POWER-UP

Uplift self and uplift others, daily.

I began my young adult life on a successful note but neglected to cultivate my mind and positive energy in a meaningful way. This oversight led to a series of hardships, including unhappy relationships, divorce, and depression. Eventually, I refocused on nurturing my positive energy and reclaimed my happiness. Just as you allocate time to earning and investing money, so too should you dedicate time to elevating your mind. Don't overlook this crucial aspect, especially when life is going smoothly. Consider it comparable to a savings account for your well-being; these "savings" will sustain you through life's challenges and contribute to a consistently happy life until the end.

Now, let's explore the what, why, and how of the Happiness Mountain approach to uplifting your life.

WHAT IS UPLIFTING?

In the context of Happiness Mountain, uplifting focuses on three key areas:

- Uplifting your daily energy and maintaining a surplus of positive energy
  - Enhancing your self-awareness
  - Uplifting others

By embarking on the journey up Happiness Mountain, you'll be enhancing your self-awareness throughout this book. In this chapter, we'll concentrate on uplifting both your energy and the energy of others.

WHY UPLIFTING IMPORTANT

Do you brush your teeth every day? Do you brush more than once? You brush daily to prevent the buildup of bacteria that occurs when you eat. For optimal dental health, brushing both in the morning and at night is recommended.

In the same way, our minds need regular cleaning. Various thoughts enter your mind daily—some positive, some negative. Daily uplifting is a mental cleanse, helping you focus on the positive. To achieve the best results, uplifting in the morning and at night is advisable. Doing so allows you to maintain a surplus of positive energy, which leads to sustainable happiness. When negative events occur, you'll have a reserve of positive energy to draw upon, preventing unnecessary suffering.

Uplifting others is comparable to cleaning your house. By improving your surroundings, you naturally create a better living environment. When you uplift those around you, they reciprocate by sending positive energy your way through their good thoughts about you.

Now, let's explore how you can practice daily uplifting for both yourself and others.

UPLIFT SELF

Are you someone who waits to complete all your tasks before finding time for a workout or meditation? This approach needs to change. Prioritize your mind and body first, and then attend to other matters. This is akin to the emergency instructions on an airplane: put on your own oxygen mask first before assisting others.

It's crucial to uplift and recharge your positive energy both in the morning and at night. If you can't spare 30 minutes to an hour in the morning, consider going to bed an hour earlier to make time for self-care. Regardless of when you wake up, begin your day by focusing on your mind and body first. Happiness Mountain recommends a **five-step morning uplifting routine**:

1 Awaken your body with some stretching or yoga moves.
2 Read your affirmations.
3 Express gratitude for what you have and the people in your life.
4 Draft your Happiness Schedule for the day.
5 Spend 5–10 minutes in meditation.

Feel free to perform these steps in any order that suits you. Doing things will help you to be more productive during the day. Your chances of getting the stress hormone cortisol will go down. You become healthier.

Importantly, approach each activity as a joyful experience, not a chore. Each step should make you feel good; if it doesn't, you're likely not in the right mindset and won't produce the "happy hormones" you're aiming for. Read the Happy Hormone section for tips on how to make these activities truly joyful experiences. For instance, stretching and yoga should make you feel good and trigger the release of serotonin. Similarly, genuine gratitude can boost your serotonin levels, while setting an exciting daily Happiness Schedule should stimulate dopamine production.

DAILY HAPPINESS SCHEDULE

Each morning or before bed, reflect on the day ahead and assess whether it feels inspiring to you. Suppose it doesn't take steps to make it so. You possess the power to shape your daily life and make it inspiring. You are the author of your own life story, so create with intention. Engage in activities you love, uplift others, and be a source of inspiration.

Here's a simple example of my Happiness Schedule for a work-from-home day:
- 5:00–5:30: Energize with my morning routine
- 5:30–7:00: Write about happiness to inspire others
- 7:00–8:00: Exercise to maintain a happy, healthy body
- 8:00–9:00: Help kids get ready for school
- 9:00–5:00: Work to contribute to my company's success
- 5:00–7:00: Enjoy dinner and family time
- 7:00–9:00: Relax with activities like yoga, sauna, or swimming
- 9:00–10:00: Read a book before bed

As you can see, my life isn't complicated, but it is fulfilling and inspiring to me. The key is to find inspiration in your daily activities. I approach each activity creatively and consciously, turning them into happy experiences that inspire me.

Affirmations

Affirmations are concise statements designed to motivate and inspire you. They serve as a powerful tool for reprogramming your mindset and inspiring a fulfilling life. Here are some Happiness Mountain affirmations you can practice daily:

- I make every experience a happy experience
- I live with full positive energy
- I live without stress and worries
- I live a joyful and balanced life
- I live with inner happiness
- I release my greatness

- I enjoy a fulfilled life with happiness, health, wealth, and doing what you love

Additionally, you can create your own list of affirmations to elevate your mindset, such as:

- I am perfect just the way I am
- I am uniquely me, and I love myself
- I am smart and intelligent enough to achieve anything I desire
- I am attracting more and more abundance simply by being the wonderful person I am
- I am confident and capable in all that I undertake

Read your affirmations every single day to shape your mind and thoughts will follow in positive direction.

UPLIFT OTHERS

I was fortunate to have an exceptional coach who uplifted me through his unwavering support. He consistently spoke positively, in stark contrast to the negativity that often pervades conversations. Successful individuals avoid associating with those who bring others down with negative talk. I'm immensely grateful to my coach for enlightening me on how to genuinely care for others. Here are some uplifting phrases from my interactions with him:

- "I think very, very highly of you."
- "I know you can do it, and I have all the faith that you'll be very successful."
- "I am very, very happy and proud of you."
- "Stay focused, and you will be very successful."
- "You are truly very special."

- "I'm very proud of your progress. You definitely have true focus now."
- "I hope you know how much I believe in you by now."
- "I'm very honored to be your coach."

Inspired by his uplifting approach, I decided to emulate him, starting with my own children. I'm now mindful of the words I use with them, offering consistent support rather than complaints and providing guidance rather than criticism. I also make it a point to spend quality time with them.

Climbing Happiness Mountain is an effective way to uplift both yourself and others. Utilize the Happiness Mountain app daily for consistent uplifting. The app is designed to reshape your mindset in the shortest time each morning. Additionally, tune into the weekly Happiness Mountain podcast available on all popular podcast platforms, and read a chapter of this book every night before bed. Make it a point to incorporate Happiness Mountain into your daily routine until it becomes a healthy habit. Think of practicing Happiness Mountain as comparable to brushing your teeth both morning and night.

CHAPTER 9
LOVE POWER-UP

*Radiate love with blessings, empathy, compassion,
kindness, and forgiveness.*

I entered into a new relationship after nine months of my separation. I continuously engaged with my former partner in parenting matters. I wanted to maintain a good relationship with her, yet it was challenging.

I heard a story from a monk: A girl goes to a temple and says "I love you" to a monk. The monk says, "I love you too." The girl went to the temple again and listened to the monk during dharma on the second day, but he said nothing to her. The girl came on the third day and got no response from the monk. Finally, she went to the monk and asked, "Why are you ignoring me and not expressing love?" The monk explained, "I said I love you. And I love everyone here as well. If someone sits under a tree to get shade from the sun, everyone can get shade. If they wear a hat, only one can get the shade. I am like a tree, and I give love to everyone that comes to me."

I realized then that I could love both of them in different contexts. This opened a new door in my mind to loving everyone.

WHAT IS LOVE?

Love has many meanings. It is desire-based love if you are strongly attracted to and love that person. What we are discussing is the love of God when you unconditionally love everyone with humanity. As human beings, we need both desire-based love and love of God among fellow human beings. Nature created us with the need for love. Humanity is based on love, both desire-based and unconditional. Let's embrace the gift of love. But why do we get angry? We came empty to this world and will depart it the same way. In between, people have many problems and forget their love for each other.

Happiness Mountain defines love as a collective feeling arising from five traits:

> Love Package = Blessings, Empathy, Compassion, Kindness, and Forgiveness.
>
> — AMAL INDI

You can send blessings as part of sending love. Blessings radiate a certain type of energy. Empathy is the ability to understand and share feelings with others. How you make other people feel is a significant part of being. Compassion is understanding the other person's suffering and having sympathy. Kindness is always about acts of kindness. Forgiving someone for their mistakes is part of your love for others. When you put them together, true love radiates from you.

WHY LOVE IS IMPORTANT

You can be a devil, a human, or a god with someone. You have the choice. The question is, Are you conscious of it?

By living with your love package, you can access the true greatness within you. Humanity is based on godly love. There is no gray line between love and anger. Wherever love is lost, it will be replaced by anger, hate, and suffering. If you want inner peace, you must live with love. There is no workaround for this universal principle. Each time you get angry, your aura changes to one of negative energy. It impacts your happiness and health. It does not matter if you justify it by saying it is for the recipient's good. Your ego and greed are enemies that prevent you from being in love. Recognize and let go of them. Live an extraordinary life with love. You do not always have to be right. You do not have to control everything. Be humble, and do not let your ego and greed take over.

Some are born with the love package. For me, this was not the case. I had to practice, and I reprogrammed myself every day. Awareness made me conscious of all five traits. I think of them during my interactions with others. The results are excellent. I am much happier in my relationships with others by using the love package.

HOW TO GIVE LOVE

Whatever prayer means to you, when you pray or send blessings you are sending love. Consider love to be your divine energy. For example, when someone is sick, you can send love and bless the other person to get well soon. If prayers and blessings associate with religious meaning to you and you do not want to use them, you can use the word "wish." You can say, "I wish them love, happiness, and good health." In either case, your good energy will propagate to the other person and help them to heal.

Empathy is understanding their feelings and the ability to share their feelings with others. When you talk to the sick person, have empathy, share your feelings, and be sensitive to theirs during difficult times. Compassion is understanding the suffering they are going through and having sympathy. Kindness is an action you can do to make another person feel better. For example, you could make soup and take it to a sick person to help them heal. During a difficult time, another person may say something wrong to you. Forgiveness is not getting upset about mistakes, and continuing to love unconditionally. Someone facing difficult times may not be at their best. You can distinguish yourself by being at your best to offer blessings, empathy, compassion, kindness, and forgiveness to make a difference in their life.

FOCUS ON HOW YOU MAKE OTHERS FEEL

What is essential during interactions with others is *how you make them feel*. If you make them feel good, you have radiated love. Human beings do not remember what you do or say. How you make them feel goes to their subconscious mind; they do not forget that for their lifetime.

 How you make others feel goes to their subconscious mind and stays forever. Always make others feel good using the love package.

For example, I shouted at my kids when they had not done their homework. That makes them feel bad. After climbing Happiness Mountain, I am always conscious about how I make them feel. I now guide them with love and do not shout at them. I now know I lack the skills to influence and guide them with loving words if I am shouting or angry. I practiced applying the love package, and now I am happy that I do not shout or get angry. It's good for my happiness and their happiness. I have the most incredible relationship with my children. I know that they will remember me as a truly loving dad. Once you use the love package, you will love it. I apply the love package to everyone. It could be my friends, former partners, work colleagues, or anyone else. When you use the love package, you can quickly radiate love and make others feel good, and, in turn, you feel good about yourself.

HOW TO HELP, OR ASK FOR IT

In life, you may find at times that you are doing well, and during others you need help. If you need help, pray or wish to receive love to overcome the challenge. Ask for help in the form of an act of kindness. If someone else needs help, spread love to them to help them heal. Help them with an act of kindness.

For example, during times of war, people suffer. You can pray to end the suffering and send your love and blessings. Donating to the Red Cross is an act of kindness. If you are helping to re-settle a family, you are performing an act of kindness with empathy and compassion. On the other hand, if you have been affected by the war and need help, ask for it from the universe or God and you will receive love from others. We all need help at some point in life. It could be during a sickness, a relationship breakup, a job loss, the impact of a natural disaster, or any other life challenge.

I send love and blessings to the world every morning during my prayers. If I know someone who is suffering, I send my love and blessings to heal them. Start your day by spreading love.

DON'T BE TRAPPED BY RESPONSIBILITY AND LOSE LOVE

I used to raise my voice to my children as a responsible dad when they spent too much time playing. I used to justify it by saying I was being responsible. Usually, a person who puts on a responsibility hat without awareness loses kindness. If you cannot show love and kindness, it negatively impacts you and others immensely. People use responsibility as an excuse to exercise power because they lack the skills to guide and influence others. As a parent, now I spend time guiding my children in their lives rather than shouting at them.

Similar things can happen in marriage or at work. One person might think their perspective is right and argue. Arguments will lead to anger and a loss of kindness. Have integrity in your relationship to maintain love and kindness, no matter what.

FORGIVENESS

> *The weak can never forgive. Forgiveness is the attribute of the strong*
>
> — MAHATMA GANDHI

Until you forgive a person you believe has done something wrong to you, you are suffering from the Anger Thought Bug, and the other person is suffering from guilt. Please remember, until you forgive, you do not have freedom. I have seen many people live with anger after relationship breakups, complaining and judging each other. My former partner and I are now best friends. She follows the Happiness Mountain program. We raise two amazing kids with love. During the divorce, we fought and hurt each other a lot. In the end, we found peace by forgiving each other. Since we have done that, our kids enjoy seeing two happy parents.

Why can't people forgive? Think about yourself. Is there someone you have not forgiven? Then you are suffering inside. Your inner happiness is impacted. Those fires are deep inside you. To find peace, you must forgive. Talk to the other person. Take responsibility for what happened. Any failure occurred with your involvement, too. Therefore, take full responsibility for your side. Then you will release the other person. If you leave one percent of the fault to the other party, you will struggle to forgive. I did not act with integrity in my marriage, so I took 100 percent responsibility for my marriage's failure.

If it is the other person's fault and you cannot forgive easily, try to be kind and forgive their mistakes by acknowledging that everyone has Thought Bugs. None of us are perfect. Remind yourself by saying:

> *I am not perfect.*
> *Others are not perfect.*
> *The world is not perfect.*
> *I bless the other person to be better and move on.*

Accept that others will do things that you do not like. What you do is maintain your values, no matter what. Bless the other person to overcome the things that you did not like. You live with the love package, forgiveness, acceptance, patience, and gratitude because those are your values. People do things because of a lack of awareness, and you might have lived similarly. Now you always live and guide others to create a better world. You live in your higher vibration by forgiving other people's words, actions, and behaviors. Do not get impacted by others and have the courage to stay in your values with Integrity. Do not criticize them, bless them.

Forgive yourself for your mistakes. I've made lots of them and learned so much and got better. Forgiveness is a tool to help you let go of the past and create a beautiful future.

Now I hope you have clarity about love. Your love package will make you beautiful, inside and out.

CHAPTER 10
ACCEPTANCE POWER-UP

Take it easy when you don't like.

WHAT IS ACCEPTANCE?

When my kids do not do things they are supposed to, such as studying instead of playing online games or not putting their dirty clothes into the laundry, I get upset, and I used to speak loudly. I lost kindness. If they were doing things right, I did not have a problem. I wanted my former partner to think the way I did and agree on things with me more than disagree. I argued if she disagreed because I believed I was right. If she agreed, I did not have a problem.

There are two possibilities of liking and happiness:

- Things that I like: I am happy
- Thinks I do not like: I am not happy

I want to increase the possibilities for my happiness. Therefore, I revised my patterns and took it easy on the things I did not like.

- Things that I like: I am happy
- Things I do not like: I take it easy

Now I can be happy 100 percent of the time. I tested it, and it worked. Now my simple definition of Acceptance is, "Acceptance is taking it easy on things that you do not like."

Right vs. wrong and good vs. bad is the default behavior of the mind. I gave up binary thinking and learned to see the neural-state option of taking it easy and not adding meanings. I became an accepting person.

WHY ACCEPTANCE IS IMPORTANT

Acceptance is your best energy saver. If you do not act with acceptance, you lose a lot of energy from the friction you create within your mind and the outer world. A lot of conflicts and disagreements start because of a lack of acceptance. Learn to accept different views. Learn to accept life's challenges. Learn to live with uncertainty by accepting it. When you start to worry, start with acceptance. You cannot control the outer world, but you can change your mind to accept it. When you do, Thought Bugs cannot creep into your mind. You preserve your positive energy to act with your greatness. You can enjoy life's gifts of peace and harmony. It is a practice. When you do it consciously a couple of times, you will start liking it, making it a habit.

HOW TO PRACTICE ACCEPTANCE

There are three types of acceptance that you can implement consciously:

- Accept yourself
- Accept other people
- Accept future uncertainty
- Accept imperfections

ACCEPT YOURSELF

Another essential part of life is accepting who you are. When you do so, you get to enjoy self-love. We all have greatness, but none of us are perfect. At times it may be hard to accept things such as past trauma, gender, sexual orientation, how you look or feel about certain parts of the body, etc. We also like certain behaviors of ours more than others. Your beautiful creation is all of them. The sooner you accept who you are, the sooner you will stop your suffering and find a place of greater happiness.

> *We all have our good side, the part of us we love. It is full of light, and we like to display it to the outside world. At the same time, we all sense that we also have a darker side. From an early age, we learn how to hide our shadow side, even suppress it, and we are nearly always unpleasantly surprised when this side of us breaks out and is revealed.*
>
> *Everything we keep locked away in our box of shadows, however, has a tendency to grow because it wants nothing more than to break free from the darkness into the light. It's as if these shadows long to be transformed by the light and become, in some wonderful*

way, aspects of ourselves that we reintegrate into our being and thus we will become whole.

— FROM THE BOOK *OUT OF THE HOLY FORCE OF LOVE* BY ANISIS

ACCEPT OTHER PEOPLE

Let us look at where the lack of acceptance comes from. You have a belief system within you. Anything that does not comply with your beliefs becomes friction within your mind unless you accept things outside this belief system. Sometimes you can get angry because another person's belief system differs from yours. You feel you are 100 percent correct. There are principles and laws in society. If it is against the law, then yes, it is wrong. Beliefs, on the other hand, are different from each other. We have to accept and respect other people's beliefs for our peace of mind. Avoid trying to be right or wrong. You can express yourself, and so can others. If you cannot agree, you can agree to disagree.

In relationships, many arguments happen because people cannot accept the other person's views. People are unique, and their belief systems are different. The easiest thing is accepting people for who they are. Accept the situation as it is. If you are unhappy in your marriage or relationship, your workplace, or in social media groups, you have not elevated your acceptance quality. I use this affirmation to reprogram my mind: "I am an accepting person. I accept people and situations the way they are."

ACCEPT FUTURE UNCERTAINTY

Life is interesting because we do not know the future. Become friends with uncertainty. Do not allow uncertainty to bring you fear. Trust that everything is going to be OK, and do your best with a positive attitude. Then everything will be OK.

ACCEPT IMPERFECTIONS

Things happen without your control, in relationships, work, society, and the world. Accept those situations. Do not resist the problem. It will invite negative energy in and block your clarity. None of us are perfect. The world is not perfect. And that is OK. Acceptance is also a gift from the universe. Open the gift.

Now, look at some imperfections in your life, in your relationship or work. Now accept them, saying, "I am not perfect, my relationship is not perfect . . . so what? I love my relationship." Do the same thing with your work. Let's be happy. The moment you do that, your happy path opens.

CHAPTER 11
PATIENCE POWER-UP

Patience is bitter, but its fruit is sweet.

—ARISTOTLE

WHAT IS PATIENCE?

I met a childhood friend and his wife after I hadn't seen them for a long time. They were having a challenging time in their marriage. I talked about good personal qualities such as love, kindness, and mindfulness. My friend's wife said patience is what saved their marriage. Then I realized patience is a very important Positive Power-Up that we possess.

Patience is the ability to wait calmly when you feel negative. When negative thoughts come to mind, do not respond immediately, and give yourself some time to calm down. For example:

- Anger Bug: Be patient and allow time to calm down before responding.

- Expectation Bug: When you expect something from someone and they do not meet the expectation, allow some time to pass before responding.
- Worry Bug: When you are going through a challenging time such as financial difficulty, losing a job, or a relationship breakup, allow some time to work it through patiently.
- Craving Bug: When strong desires come to mind, be patient and do not respond immediately. Then make a conscious decision. You will see that your mind calms down and the strong need goes away.

WHY IS PATIENCE IMPORTANT?

If you act with negative energy, you are not making the best choice. If you continue to do that, you will accumulate problems in life. If you want to live a happy and peaceful life, learn to be patient. If you want to have great relationships, patience is a must-have quality. If you are losing patience, you might say or do something negative you cannot take back. There is no easy delete button. What you say or do changes the energy around you. If you create negative energy, you need to make an effort to rectify it back into positive energy. You will be far better positioned by not reacting and giving some time before saying or doing something while you are in a negative state.

HOW TO BE PATIENT

You have heard the saying that "time heals all wounds." Therefore, give it some time. We all go through many things in our heads. We need to provide some space and time to heal. Be conscious of the following scenarios:

- Handling misunderstandings
- While listening

- Facing uncertainty

DEALING WITH THOUGHT BUGS

When you feel negative, Patience is the best tool to let time heal your mind and the situation. In Part Three, you will learn how to deal with Negative Thoughts Bugs patiently.

HANDLING MISUNDERSTANDINGS

Most relationship issues arise because of misunderstandings and miscommunication. You can usually talk over these misunderstandings. If you are experiencing negative energy, wait until you feel positive before patiently responding. You have to use acceptance (take it easy when you do not like it) and patience (allow some time together when you feel negative).

Consider acceptance and patience as a combo Power-Up. Learn to operate together, and you will have protection from negative energy. After you feel calm, you can address the real issue, whatever it is.

TECHNIQUE: 24-HOUR PASS

A good technique that can be used is to wait for 24 hours without thinking about the matter. Patiently wait until you have one good sleep before responding.

HANDLING MISUNDERSTANDINGS WHILE LISTENING

Listening consciously to another person requires patience. I find this very useful, particularly in meetings at work or when I am in an argument. When your mind wants to jump in and say your opinion is correct, you must step back, listen to others, and share your opinion. Patience helps you not to talk over the other person. Patience with consciousness allows you to understand what the other person says.

WHILE FACING UNCERTAINTY

Our untrained minds do not like uncertainty. There could be situations where they create uncertainty about the future—for example, bad economic situations, political unrest, job precariousness, health, or security after retirement. The untrained mind wants security to feel happy. In the dynamic world, we cannot always expect security but we can train our minds to accept uncertainty. You have to trust the universe, the creator, or God, whatever that means to you. God always loves you. Ask for guidance from God, believe everything will be OK, and then take positive action. The script that I use is: "Dear God, please show me the path to [what you want to resolve] and many more happy years to come."

You do not have to control everything about the future. Trust the universe and believe that everything is going to be OK.

CHAPTER 12
MODERATION POWER-UP

Let go of strong attachments, frictions, or judgments.

There have been various periods in my life: I was a workaholic, deeply in love, obsessed with casual sex, and running after goals to become successful. Almost all of them brought down my balance. I did not practice moderation. Moderation was not in my value system before climbing Happiness Mountain. The outcome was I had only temporary happiness and was suffering within myself with worry and stress. I was living an unfulfilled life.

WHAT IS MODERATION?

Your mind makes three primary thought patterns:

1. **Attachment:** Your mind tends to attach to people, opinions, and desires.

2. **Friction:** Your mind tends to create friction with people, opinions, or desires.
3. **Judge:** Your mind tends to judge people, opinions, or desires.

Moderation is your state of mind when you let go of strong attachments, frictions, or judgments concerning people, opinions, and desires. You develop skills to observe thoughts and take it easy. The next step is to adjust your thoughts to let go, and your speech and actions will automatically align to avoid strong attachments, frictions, or judgments.

WHY MODERATION IS IMPORTANT

When you are practicing moderation, you become conscious. If you are not moderating, you attract negative energy. If you do not practice moderation, your mind cannot be kept calm and strong. You will always have to struggle within your mind. Your outer self might be seen as OK, but your inner self will suffer. Without moderation, there is no inner happiness. You cannot live a phenomenal and happy life. Most of the time we ignore the value and power of moderation.

HOW TO EXERCISE MODERATION

The following are scenarios that a Moderation Power-Up can be applied to in order to live a happy life.

- Opinions and arguments
- Desires
- Suppression vs. moderation
- Future success vs. today's happiness
- Overthinking

OPINIONS AND ARGUMENTS

Different people have different opinions and beliefs. We all need to understand that and learn to respect others' views. When you come across an argument based on these opinions and beliefs, do not try to prove you are right; instead, be moderate and share your views but do not try to prove you are correct. Everyone else works the same way, trying to prove they are right. Happiness resides in respecting and sharing each other's beliefs rather than convincing others that you are right. Stick to your beliefs, and at the same time learn to respect others'. That is a simple principle to create a happier life. If you break this principle, suffering will follow you.

When you observe that you are attaching to an opinion or creating friction with another person's opinion, your break is applying moderation.

Your homework is to practice moderation in your engagements with people. Do not attach, cause friction or judge. At the beginning of the interaction, say to yourself that you are powering up moderation and observe your speech. Take more pauses, ask questions, and let the other person talk. Make sure you are talking without strong attachments, frictions, or judgments. As soon as you see you are attaching to your own opinions, or that you are in friction with the other person's views, consciously come to moderation again.

DESIRES

We all love dopamine, which is triggered by pleasure or achievements. You have life goals and achievements to fulfill. Those need your dopamine. Pleasure also creates dopamine. If you entertain too much dopamine with pleasure activities, your mind is happy with them and will not be motivated to do the things that matter in life. For example, someone who experiences casual-sex-related dopamine cannot have a successful committed relationship. I am not saying these are right or wrong, I am saying this is what happens to your mind. If you want a happy, healthy, wealthy, and beautiful life, make up your mind about your obsessions. I did it without impacting my happiness. I practiced moderation, stepped back, and then replaced the areas where my dopamine was triggered. Dopamine from fulfillment is cleaner and way more pleasurable than taking happiness dopamine from obsessions like alcohol, porn, casual sex, games, excess food, and drugs.

SUPPRESSION VS. MODERATION

Consider obsessions as blockers to your life's success. You can suppress obsession. It works sometimes, but it may not work as well. It is better to have awareness and replace obsessions. Suppression will most likely not be sustainable, and you will return to them again. It's all about your dopamine-related pleasure and achievements. If you lack dopamine pleasure for weeks, your mind may not feel happiness. Chances are you'll be drawn back to your obsession.

My experience is that if you let go of your obsessions, you need to be leading a spiritual life. Then it is easy because you are at peace and have minimal desires. I tried this, and it worked very well for my obsessions. But the issue is we live an everyday life with work, kids, friends, and family. Chances are you are drawn to pleasures as well. How do we let go of our obsessions in regular life? The answer is moderation, replacement, and letting go. Replace your desires with something you love that is healthy. Your passion. Your life's purpose. Enjoy nature. Enjoy life in a balance of dopamine, serotonin, oxytocin, and endorphins.

FUTURE SUCCESS VS TODAY'S HAPPINESS

I have seen many people suffering from their great desires today for future success. The Happiness Mountain philosophy is to be happy today and create success while being in a balanced life. If you do many good things without a balanced life, you are not on the correct happiness path. Then you could feel stressed, even when doing good things. There is no way to have a happy and successful life without balance. I do many fulfilling pursuits within a balanced life. No matter what, I stay connected with nature; I spend time with my family, and I enjoy time for myself. I never break my daily balance. With moderation, your mind is at peace. If you do an excess of anything, you will lose your peace of mind.

OVERTHINKING

Your mind may sometimes want to overthink problems, such as financial stability, retirement, your children's future, health, or physical appearance. Overthinking and over-worrying is not good for your happiness. You have to trust the universe and be moderate in your worrying. Be moderate and patient. Let time resolve things. Focus and be happy today. Live a balanced life in moderation.

CHAPTER 13
MINDFULNESS POWER-UP

Focus 100 percent on the simple activity you are doing right now.

WHAT IS MINDFULNESS?

I use mindfulness as a happiness tool. To enjoy life to the fullest, you have to become mindful. For example:

- Don't just talk, listen
- Don't just look, observe
- Don't just eat, taste
- Don't just shower, feel
- Don't just work, create
- Don't just exist, live

You are mindful when you are focused on the current activity without wandering inside your head with unintentional thoughts. One of the highest levels of happiness you can achieve is being present in the moment. You are not mindful if you think or multitask other things while doing the current activity. When you perform your daily activities mindfully, you get a bonus capability: Your conscious mind gets activated. What is the importance of the conscious mind? You can make the best decisions toward your success. You do not become enslaved to thoughts. If you are a slave of your thoughts, you lose happiness quickly when a worry comes to your mind. With those worry thoughts, you can suffer from your own mind. With mindfulness you can be at peace, even during challenging times.

WHY MINDFULNESS IS IMPORTANT

Your brain is crucial for your happiness. It is an organ that needs good care while operating during the day. The mind is more than a physical organ, and the brain plays a significant role in having a happy mind. It is helpful for you to understand the basics of brain waves and how they operate during different states of being. Brain wave samples for different waveforms are shown below.

HUMAN BRAIN WAVES

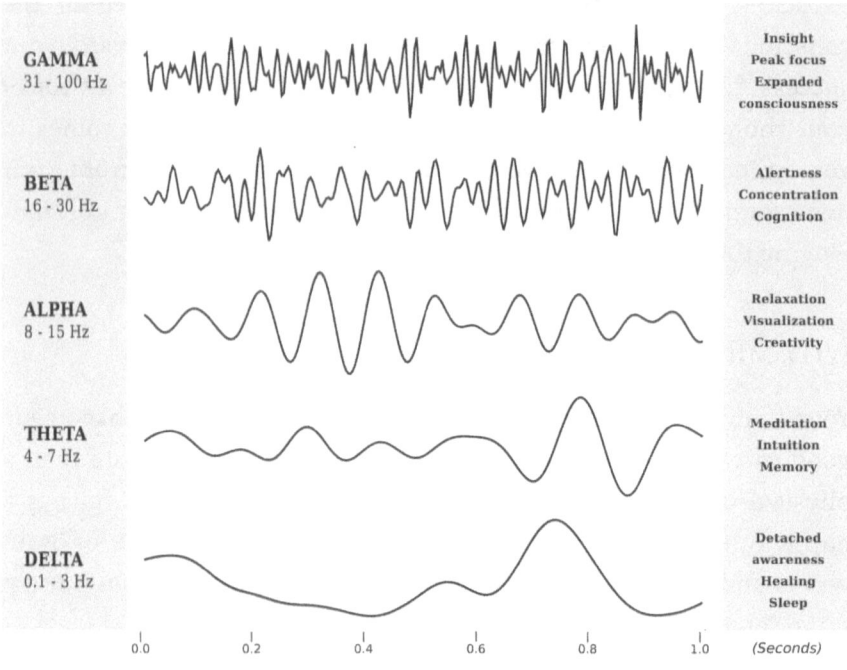

Brain Waves

When you are busy, the brain operates at the beta range. When you are mindful, you go to alpha ranges, a very relaxed state. When you are focused, you go to gamma ranges in which you can do creative work with expanded consciousness. The brain should operate at delta ranges with proper sleep for your recovery. Theta is a passive inward focus state that you go to before you sleep, or you can get to that range with extended meditation.

The way I remember different brain wage ranges is:

- Increase self-concentration and do creative work with the gamma range
- Avoid high beta range by not being too busy

- Be restful in the alpha range with mindfulness
- Deep relaxation with theta with extended meditation
- Get enough sleep to rest the brain in the delta range

Brain waves are the result of how you live your day. Focus on living every day mindfully and avoid being too busy, and your brain will work accordingly to your advantage.

HOW TO BECOME MINDFUL

The following are the fundamental principles of becoming mindful:

- Slow down
- Live in the moment
- Have an intention for every experience
- Connect with your breath
- Connect with energy and heal yourself
- Mediate

SLOW DOWN

When you slow down physical activity, you become naturally mindful. Try to eat slowly. See what happens. Suddenly, you realize that you have become conscious. Try to drink water slowly. Talk slowly with pauses when you are in a conversation. You will suddenly realize that you are connected to the present moment.

Slow is smooth, smooth is fast.

— US NAVY SEALS

Conscious slowness is a practical and powerful trick to train your mind to become mindful in daily activities. Stop rushing in life. Train your mind to be grounded by adding slowness to your activities. You will achieve your goals faster by adding extra slowness in the present moment because you are more conscious. You can see things clearly. Your mind does not get tired. You live with your natural rhythm.

LIVE IN THE MOMENT

Living mindfully means you are living in the present moment, and you pay complete attention to the activity you are involved in. This means you are not living in the past or the possible future. How do you do this even though you physically live in the present moment? This happens with thought chains. When you can overcome thought chains and connect to the present moment, you will experience mindfulness. Living in the moment gives you a remarkably high level of happiness. You can stay in the moment by:

- Giving 100 percent focus to the current activity
- Keeping your thoughts related to the activity
- Stopping any multitasking

HAVE AN INTENTION FOR EVERY EXPERIENCE

Intentions move you to act in the right direction. Without intentions, your mind is not focused. As soon as you set the intention for the activity, your mind connects to it.

Your day is a collection of experiences.

- Enjoy the experiences by making them happy ones
- Undertake experiences with love and passion
- Set intentions before starting any experience

For example, when I cook dinner I make it a happy experience with some music, and I enjoy the cooking. I do it with love and passion. My intention is to happily make a healthy meal for my family. What I do not do anymore is a "daily task that I have to do." I overcame this by practicing Happiness Mountain methodology.

Use your master intention of "making every experience a happy experience" daily. Use it as a base to create a custom intention for the experience. For example, if you are going to a meeting, you can set an intention of happily achieving what you want in the meeting. Always add "happily" to the intention. The mind will receive clear instructions to engage in the experience. Otherwise, it will wander around without knowing what to do. Wandering leads to a lack of interest, and you will start multitasking. Start intention-driven life for everything you do. Intentions will help to reduce random thoughts coming to mind. That simple habit will change your life, and you will be happier in everything you do.

CONNECT WITH YOUR BREATH

Breath is your anchor to staying mindful. When you connect to your breath, you can prevent your mind from going into deep thought chains. The trick to staying in the present moment is connecting to the breath. The mind needs something to stick to. Use that stickiness to connect with the breath; do not wander inside your head. Breathe deeply. Feel the cool air flowing into your lungs and rib cage. Hold it for a few seconds. Release it and feel the warm air leaving. Hold it again at the end. Practice getting into the habit of being aware of your breath, and your mindfulness will increase.

CONNECT WITH ENERGY AND HEAL YOURSELF

Another way to become mindful is by connecting with your energy and the energy surrounding you. For example, when you shower, feel the water on your skin rather than thinking about work or other things going on in your life. Feel the temperature and tingle of the water and connect with its energy, and the energy within you. Once you master mindfulness, you can use the energy around you to heal.

Practice mindfulness and heal your mind and body with the energy from nature.

When I wake up, I go outside and heal my mind and body with the fresh morning energy from nature. This is an excellent way to feel energy and become mindful.

MEDITATE

There are many types of meditation, and they are all good for you. Here are some of the meditations you can practice:

- Focused meditation helps you become more centered.
- Mindfulness waking meditation helps you to become present in daily activities.
- Calming meditation: Listen to meditative music to calm the mind.
- Clearance meditation: Observe thoughts and learn to separate yourself from them.
- Body-scanning meditation improves your mindfulness.
- Meditating with affirmations reprograms your mind and supports your goals.

Join Happiness Mountain meditation sessions that you can find on the Happiness Mountain website. You can also use the Happiness Mountain app to practice. There are specialized meditation apps that you can try as well.

Your inner world is the life inside your head, filled with thoughts and stories created by your mind. If the concept of your thoughts being separate from your true self is new to you, I would like to offer you a clearance meditation that you can try in your own time.

 Find a comfortable and calm place to sit. Ensure your phone is turned to silent and you have five minutes to yourself. This will allow you to be in your own space for a moment. This can be at home, in a quiet space at work, or outdoors. Close your eyes and listen to the surrounding sounds. Your mind will automatically begin going into your thoughts about the day, work, something that happened, things you need to do, etc. When you recognize that your mind is focusing on your thoughts, let the thoughts return to the surrounding sounds. You may do this several times. Dive into your thoughts, then repeat, "Random thoughts are just thoughts. They mean nothing," and once again return to listening to your surroundings. You will realize how many thoughts come to mind. Slowly bring your focus to the breath. Start enjoying the peace of being connected to your breath.

An important outcome of meditation is distinguishing between your thoughts and yourself. Thoughts are not you, but inner talk appears like you. When you are meditating, you can make this distinction easily. Do not let random thoughts control your life. You will learn intention-driven thought in later chapters.

TIPS TO GETTING STARTED:

1. Understand what mindfulness is and why it is so important to happiness.
2. Always remember that "slow is smooth and smooth is fast."
3. The brain is an organ that needs relaxation and sleep.
4. Be in the alpha range with mindfulness. Avoid the high beta range.

5. When you wake up, go outside and mindfully feel the air and nature.
6. Go for a walk while observing the outdoors and feel the nature around you.
7. Eat slowly and taste the food.
8. Focus on feeling the water when you shower or bathe.
9. When you exercise, feel the energizing effects on your body.
10. When you walk, feel your body's movement and connection as you touch the earth.
11. Meditate daily for 5–20 minutes.
12. Set intention and stay present. Avoid multitasking.
13. Take time to do nothing. Get used to silence and peace.
14. Join happiness meditation sessions conducted by Happiness Mountain.

Experience your life to your fullest by being mindful.

CHAPTER 14
INTEGRITY POWER-UP

Live with integrity and honor.

I have been hearing about integrity as the primary success quality for a long time. I did not understand it until I climbed Happiness Mountain. I noticed a few things blocking me from going up to the top. I could see the path, but I slipped down repeatedly. In the back of my mind, I knew that integrity was the most crucial thing. Therefore, I spent time understanding it in more detail.

WHAT IS INTEGRITY?

The Oxford Dictionary definition of integrity is: "The quality of being honest and having strong moral principles; moral uprightness."

This is a great definition, but to be honest, at first I could not understand how to implement integrity in my life with this explanation. Therefore, I dug deeper so I could know how to apply it to my life. To understand further, I asked my coach what integrity means to him. He said,

 "You live according to your deepest values, are honest with everyone, and always keep your word."

Based on his answer, I learned that Integrity has three essential elements:

1. **Live according to your deepest values and principles.** I want to die knowing that I lived with integrity and honor. Yes, I made mistakes, and that is OK. I forgave myself. By living with 100 percent integrity, I know I can die in peace. Make sure your values and principles are following love and kindness for other human beings.
2. **Be honest with everyone.** Honesty and authenticity are essential characteristics that define who you are.
3. **Always keep your word.** This is vital to your integrity. When you make a promise, you should be able to keep it. Learn to say no if you are not confident that you can keep your word. Consciously start doing this, and it will reflect positively on your life. Do not make promises to yourself or others that you cannot keep.

WHY INTEGRITY IS IMPORTANT

Integrity is directly associated with the success of what you want to do. For example, if you're going to lose weight, you must follow a nutrition plan with integrity. If you want to be a good human being, follow Happiness Power-Ups with integrity. To live a happy, healthy, and wealthy life, climb Happiness Mountain level by level with integrity. If you are going to have a good relationship, have integrity in it.

Warren Buffett is a successful American businessman and

investor with a net worth of over a hundred billion dollars. I listened carefully to what he said about integrity:

 In looking for people to hire, you look for three qualities: integrity, intelligence, and energy. And if you don't have the first, the other two will kill you.

— WARREN BUFFETT

As you can see, integrity is important for everything you do, including your work. A person who lives with good values and principles is fundamental to the success of an organization or family, or anything you do.

HOW TO ESTABLISH INTEGRITY

Train your mind for integrity in the selected area of your life, then add more and more areas. Here are three good areas in which you can become conscious of integrity as the starting point:

- Daily schedule
- Uplifting habits
- The integrity of the people in your life

DAILY SCHEDULE

My coach mentioned that the first thing I should do is have a schedule, then have complete integrity in it. I used to change my schedule throughout the day as things would come to my mind, and I would lose the integrity to do what I said I would. To create a successful life, you should have a daily schedule and the integrity to follow it.

UPLIFTING HABITS

You need to develop new habits to create a happy and successful life. The time when you set the start of the new habit is not in your body memory, and you need to put extra focus. For example, you want to limit your calorie intake and add a daily walk to lose weight. This is the time you need the Integrity Power-up. Integrity with willpower will take you to the next level. Once it becomes a habit, you do not need the extra effort. Make sure you make the new habit a happy experience. Otherwise, you will not sustain.

INTEGRITY OF THE PEOPLE IN YOUR LIFE

You may get into conflicts and experience painful moments with people. You might keep dealing with those people and stop repeatedly getting upset and angry. You should have integrity in yourself and let go of people who do not. I will share one of my experiences with an editor. She has very high skills with a lot of experience. Because of that, I hired her to do the editing of the book. But she did not respond to e-mails or deliver on time. Before I knew integrity, I tried to deal with her to solve the problem. It took a lot of energy, and I had to manage my Anger Thought Bug. After reading Warren Buffet's statement that he does not hire people without integrity, even if they have intelligence, I realized that the person I was dealing with did not have integrity in their work. So, I decided to end the service by taking a loss immediately. That released me from the burden, and I felt great. New opportunities opened for me. If you want a happy and successful life, deal with people with integrity. And make sure you live with integrity.

If you find yourself dealing with someone who does not have integrity, follow this formula:

- Discuss what you agreed to re-establish integrity.
- If you cannot come to an agreement, end with gratitude.

- Let go of all your expectations of that relationship. Take complete ownership of any blame for engaging with people without integrity and release the other person from any blame.
- Do not judge the person.

You should not create any negative energy with the other person for lacking integrity in the relationship with you. It does not mean that that they are a bad person. There could be many good reasons why they did not approach you with integrity. Since you are a person with integrity, you do not deal with people without it for the sake of your sanity and happiness. It would be best if you let the universe take care of them, whatever they have done. This is a double-edged sword, so be careful when using it. Otherwise, you could hurt other people. Always work with gratitude.

To create a happy and successful life, first establish integrity. Start focusing on different areas, as I did with my schedule and the people in my life. If you want to live a happy, successful life, surround yourself with people with integrity and be one of them.

BE AUTHENTIC

Authenticity and integrity go hand in hand. Authenticity requires you to be true to yourself.

Put simply, authenticity means you are true to your personality, values, and spirit, regardless of the pressure that you're under to act otherwise. Your values, ideals, and actions align. As a result, you will come across as genuine.

People tend to live the way others want them to when they are under social pressure. There could be many scenarios where you pretend something to your outer world, but your inner world is moving in a different direction. This false behavior takes away your happiness. Being authentic is not easy at times. It takes courage.

Once you become authentic, your internal friction goes away and you feel free and happy inside out.

The next part of authenticity is about honesty and taking responsibility for your mistakes. Be honest and resolve the issue whenever you have a conflict with someone. Your ego will try to prevent that. Overcome ego and solve problems in life with authenticity. You will find happiness in no time.

Be yourself, authentically. With integrity and authenticity, you can have sustainable happiness.

Happiness Experience Two: Living Without Stress or Worry

CHAPTER 15
EIGHT THOUGHT BUGS®: TRIGGERS OF NEGATIVE ENERGY

The first step toward happiness is to defeat negative thoughts. Negative thoughts steal most of your happiness and success, but you may not identify them. Your barrier to stopping negative energy is your lack of understanding of negative thoughts.

When I went through my divorce, I created negative energy in my life, my kids' lives, and my former spouse's life. When I got rid of this energy, I was able to create a great relationship with everyone, including my ex-wife. Now she is truly my best friend, and we raise our kids with love and have happy lives.

Our children can see that their parents are happy and prosperous and live in harmony with respect and love. I believe if you are divorced and have kids, your former partner is going to be family no matter what, as there is a lifelong relationship through the children. You are not husband and wife, but you are family. For our children, we want to create a happy family life. Children need stability, love, and guidance. We all have our paths. Every family does not have to be the same. The most important aspect is to create a happy family life, regardless of your unique situation. Accept your path as the best one for you and your family. Make it happy, unique, and remarkable for yourself, your children, and your former partner. I guarantee that, with the understanding of your negative thoughts, you can achieve this with ease. This is one of the examples that may or may not apply to you, and you can use the understanding of negative thoughts, a.k.a. Thought Bugs, in any area of your life to find peace, happiness, and joy.

LIFE CHALLENGES

In life we have good periods and challenging periods. That is the duality of life that no one can avoid. What we can do is have a strong and resilient mind to face them. Here are some examples of life challenges that could impact your happiness at some point in life:

- Relationship breakups
- Living in an unhappy relationship under the same roof
- Not having a relationship
- Divorce
- Raising kids in collaboration (or not) with your ex-partner
- Health challenges
- Getting old and uncertainty around old age
- Unhappiness with your work
- Losing the job, or fear of losing it
- Financial hardships
- Natural disasters, such as pandemics, floods, fire
- Worrying about the future, such as retirement or children's education
- Conflicts
- Confusion with spirituality and the meaning of life
- Addictions, such as drugs, alcohol, pornography, and casual sex
- Gender- or sexual-orientation-related worries

- Stress from businesses or start-ups
- Loss of loved ones

It is a superb skill if you know how to defeat negative thoughts during challenging times. Then you have more positive energy to face the challenge and build back your happy life.

WHAT ARE THOUGHT BUGS

In computer programming, a software bug is a piece of code that does not work as intended. Similarly, there are human thought patterns that we all have that do not give us the intended result of happiness. I call them Negative-Thought Bugs. Thoughts shape our life. Most people know that anger creates negative energy. There are many other negative thoughts in addition to anger. If you want to get over your negative energy, the first thing to do is identifying different Thought Bugs. I will put them into three types based on how they impact your happiness.

HARD HAPPINESS-KILLERS

- Anger Thought Bug
- Worry Thought Bug

Anger and Worry Thought Bugs kill your happiness quickly, and you can identify them easily. The most common problem is that people look at hard killers and try to address them without knowing their root cause. Usually, anger and worry are a result of another Thought Bug.

SILENT HAPPINESS-KILLERS

- Expectation Thought Bug

- Craving Thought Bug

Expectation and Craving Thought Bugs are very subtle. The Expectation Thought Bug is where you put expectations on others. In my marriage, I used to put expectations on my wife. They became the culprit of our unhappiness. Parents push expectations on their children. When things do not work out as expected, problems begin and we begin hurting each other. There are better ways to do this than putting expectations on others. We will cover this in a later chapter.

Cravings are not only about food.

Craving *n.* [1]

An intense, urgent, or abnormal desire or longing

a craving for chocolate

a craving for new experiences

Cravings are strong desires that you act on for happiness. They appear to offer joy but bring failures if not managed with awareness. Cravings can become blind spots because you are getting happiness out of them. For example, people cheat for happiness, which can end in a terrible divorce, or you may live with your wife under the same roof with unhappiness towards each other. Because of Thought Bugs, people lose the great life they once had.

SOFT HAPPINESS-KILLERS

- Judgmental Thought Bug
- Fear Thought Bug
- Self-limiting Thought Bug
- Do-It-Later Thought Bug

Soft-killer Thought Bugs are those that kill your happiness softly. You may know what they are, but you do not sufficiently notice them as problems that create unhappiness and failures. They remove the power from your day-to-day life. They can drain most of your energy.

If you are in a relationship, you have disagreements at times. After disagreements, your mind tends to complain and judge. This is common in marriages because people have not understood the difference between male and female energies. Let's say the male energy is looking at the male view with logic and trying to be responsible and right. The female energy looks at the female view, where the woman wants to be heard to ensure their opinions are respected and to achieve equality in their ideas. Then they judge each other based on opposing viewpoints, living life looking in different directions and failing to see each other. Those moments impact love and intimacy. The Anger and Judgmental Thought Bugs arrive, then the Worry Thought Bug joins in. When partners lose love and intimacy, it could lead to cheating and looking for love from outside. This could impact the whole marriage, creating a lot of negative energy.

You must understand the fundamentals of male and female energies for a healthy relationship. If you live with a partner, you have the power to create a loving and intimate relationship, irrespective of the past. Fix the fundamentals by achieving a state of awareness as a starting point. If you are looking in opposite directions and arguing in your marriage or relationship, please read the book *Men Are from Mars, Women Are from Venus* by John Gray.

Our minds like to have certainty in everything, but life is full of uncertainty. Fear Thought Bugs are waiting for uncertain moments to take your energy out of you. When you procrastinate on something, your Do-it-Later Thought Bug springs into action.

Thoughts Bugs are indeed bad, with Self-Limiting Thought Bugs being the worst. They are self-imposed limitations with thoughts such as *I am not good enough, nobody loves me*, and other self-limiting thoughts. They are programmed during your childhood. Everyone picks something from the childhood environment they were in. As adults, we should be able to recognize and overcome those self-limiting negative thoughts. Otherwise, you will live the course of your life without knowing what programs are slowing you down.

The Self-Limiting Thought Bug chapter will teach you how to recognize and overcome them systematically.

SPOT THEM TO STOP THEM

 When you spot Thought Bugs, you can stop them.

Collectively, these Thought Bugs can kill your happiness with each new day. Once you understand them, you can spot and stop them impacting your happiness. As human beings engaging in life activities, it is normal the get the Thought Bugs. The important thing is stopping them immediately so they don't impact your happiness and others'.

Happiness Experience Two of the book covers:

- how to spot them,
- how to quickly stop the power of them
- how to apply long-term solutions to get rid of them from your life

Once you master these eight Thought Bugs, your mind will not hurt you with negative thoughts. You will be able to separate your thoughts from yourself. Even when you get a negative Thought Bug, you will know how to get over it in a minimum amount of time and increase the amount of time you live happily. Time is the most valuable aspect of life. I am sure you do not want to waste time in unhappiness.

Self-awareness empowers you to live the rest of your life happier. I recommend you read each Thought Bugs chapter mindfully, since the time you spend is an investment in your happiness for the rest of your life.

CHAPTER 16
HOW TO SPOT AND STOP THOUGHT BUGS®

When I was working in the corporate office environment, concrete steps were established for troubleshooting the more common problems. In banking, this outlines the process for troubleshooting a customer problem when there is a system error in a customer's bank transfer:

- Listen to the customer and record the issue
- Investigate where the issue is
- Find the root cause
- Fix the problem
- Test that the error is genuinely resolved
- Monitor and make sure it does not happen again
- Update the customer and apologize for the error
- Close the issue

As you can see, the troubleshooting process is well structured. In comparison, here is how I typically used to deal with anger at someone:

- I did not acknowledge the anger issue
- I blamed the other person
- I worried about it for many days
- The conflict was never fully resolved
- When another incident occurred, I would get angry again
- The cycle repeated

As you can probably guess, this reactive behavior pattern led to many personal issues. I was constantly coming up against the same problems in dealing with my anger and never actually resolving them.

I asked: Why not apply a systematic approach to troubleshooting worries? Worries occur from your negative energy. I developed a troubleshooting model to manage my worries, much like the troubleshooting system at the bank. I could now approach each obstacle with ease and grace. Once you establish a system, you do not have to overthink. Just follow the steps and you get the benefits.

COMPUTER VS. HUMAN MIND

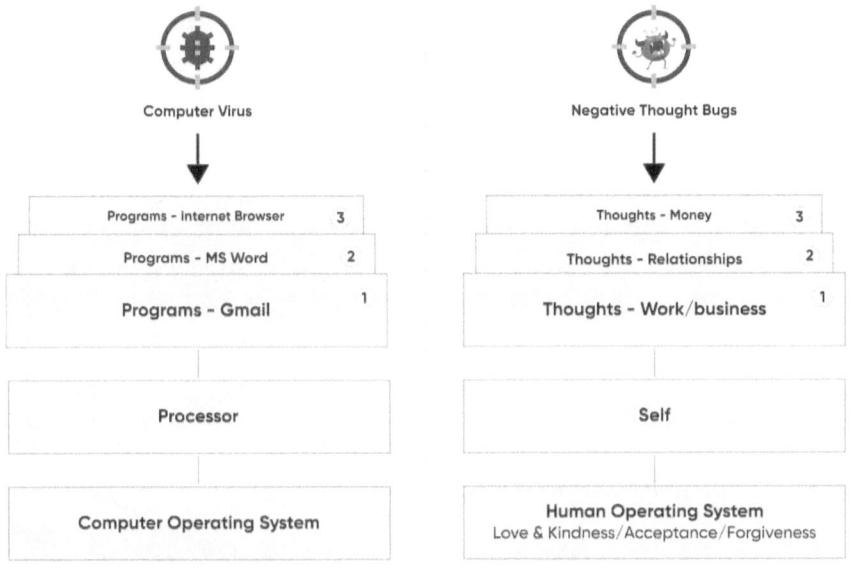

Computer vs. Human Mind

I love to compare our minds to computers; computers are a manifestation of humans and parallel our thinking in several ways. When you purchase a new computer, there is a processor, SSD drive, graphics card, operating system, programs, etc. However, installing a reliable virus scanner is left up to the user.

Viruses in our computers can take on many forms, potentially damaging them, including affecting the hardware. A virus can cause the computer to malfunction.

I find this to be the same when looking at our minds. Think of your mind as a computer—you have a processor that I relate to your decision-making power. You are born with a unique human operating system of love, compassion, kindness, acceptance, forgiveness, patience, etc. In addition, there are many programs running at the same time, like your work, cooking dinner, going to the gym, or spending time with a loved one. The programs are your thoughts.

What if a virus were to come along and interfere with these programs, interrupting the flow and hindering you from being the best person you can be? Thought Bugs are much like computer viruses, and can affect your mind.

Thought Bugs can destroy the foundation of your greatness. The majority of people in the world suffer from negative energy created by their minds. This energy created by Thought Bugs will block your potential to lead a happy and fulfilling life. If you do not take control of your Thought Bugs, your mind will suffer from them for your whole life.

THOUGHT BUGS DEFEATING SYSTEM

Consider the "Thought Bugs Defeating System" as your virus scanner for negative thoughts. Unlike millions of computer viruses, you have to master how to clean only eight Thought Bugs. Imagine how beautiful your life will be when the following negative thoughts do not make you suffer:

- Anger: Anger Thought Bug
- Worry: Worry Thought Bug
- Expectations: Expectation Thought Bug
- Strong desires (cravings & obsessions): Craving Thought Bug
- Being judgmental: Judgmental Thought Bug
- Fear (caused by suspicion): Fear Thought Bug
- Self-limiting beliefs: Self-Limiting Thought Bug
- Procrastination: Do-it-Later Thought Bug

Now let's go over the three steps to overcoming negative thoughts:

- **Step 1:** Spot the bug
- **Step 2:** Stop the bug
- **Step 3:** Assess, and complete

STEP 1: SPOT THE BUG

My brother was one of the beta readers of this book. By reading it, he understood that Thought Bugs are an essential concern to address. Rather than dealing with them daily, he realized that he wanted to address them directly.

 Defeating Thought Bugs was the turning point in my life.

— CHANAKA

Chanaka was able to find peace and increase happiness within his family tremendously by understanding and defeating Thought Bugs.

STEP 2: STOP THE BUG

Power-Ups help you to stop the negative energy arising from Thought Bugs. You can use all eight Power-Ups and see which works for your situation. There are recommended Power-Ups for each Thought Bug as your starting point.

Negative Thought Bugs	Recommended Power-Up
Worry Thought Bug	Mindfulness
Anger Thought Bug	Patience
Expectation Thought Bug	Acceptance
Craving Thought Bug	Moderation
Judgmental Thought Bug	Love
Self-Limiting Thought Bug	Inspiration
Fear Thought Bug	Gratitude
Do-it-Later Thought Bug	Integrity

Thought Bugs vs. Positive Power-Ups

Power-Ups create positive energy that is required to stop the negative energy that was generated by Thought Bugs.

STEP 3: ASSESS AND COMPLETE

In this step, you look deeper into your Thought Bugs and understand why they occur. The intention of this step is to stop the same Thought Bug from reoccurring in the future by proper root-cause analysis. Having a good understanding of why the Thought Bug was triggered and completing the root-cause analysis will help you to prevent them coming back again.

PRIORITIZE THE TOP THREE

You most likely have a few primary negative thought patterns, which I recommend focusing on first. My top three were the Cravings Thought Bug, the Expectations Thought Bug, and the Do-it-Later Thought Bug. My brother defeated his Anger Thought Bug first, and he also realized that his Expectation Thought Bug was causing the anger. So, he defeated both together. Usually, Thought Bugs come as packages consisting of one to three negative thought patterns. Here are a few examples:

- **Expectation, Judgmental, and Anger Thought Bug package**: Someone does not meet your expectations, so you start judging them and your anger joins in.
- **Do-it-Later and Worry Thought Bug package**: You procrastinate and then worry about the negative results.
- **Craving and Worry Thought Bug package**: You fulfill a strong desire and then become worried about what you did.
- **Fear and Worry Thought Bug package**: You feel uncertain of your future, causing fear, and then worry about a future that has not happened.
- **Self-Limiting and Anger Thought Bug package**: Childhood trauma triggers you, and you get angry and do not trust people, which prevents your ability to build strong relationships.
- **Self-Limiting and Worry Thought Bug package**: Your mind says, "I am not good enough," and you cannot do what you want to. You may live your whole life trapped in this negative pattern.

Now it is your turn to write your top negative thought patterns and related Thought Bugs. Try to catch one to three predominant Thought Bugs for two weeks. Set your mind to do this as a fourteen-day bug-defeating challenge. By doing fourteen days straight, you reprogram your mind to defeat them. Once reprogrammed, it will become a habit and you will not have to put in the extra effort, as you do now. After that, catching Thought Bugs becomes second nature.

CHAPTER 17
WORRY THOUGHT BUG

Worry Thought Bug

T he Worry Bug is a Hard Happiness-Killer. When you are worrying, you cannot be happy. What is a worry? It is a how our minds dwell on troubles or problems based on our experiences and reasoning. Humans are designed for survival, meaning we seek potential troubles or problems. When you engage in day-to-day activities you get worries at times, and it is normal. The skill you need to acquire is to recognize worry and stop it without getting to the stress zone. Once you know how to stop worries, you do not have to suffer from them. Let the worries come, take the counter-actions, and clear them immediately.

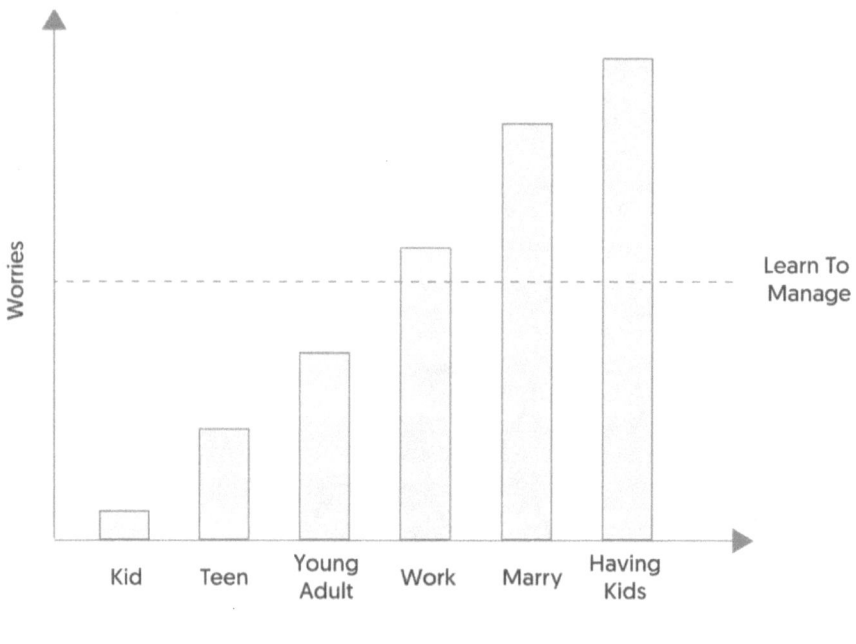

Life without negative-energy management

As outlined in the diagram above, you can clearly see how your worry will naturally increase over time. It also shows your levels of worry when you do not have the proper management tools and have not done personal development to understand your own mind.

As you can see, your worries can easily surpass your level of manageable stress (the dotted line). This creates a cycle of negative worries constantly feeding itself to become larger. Levels of worry that outgrow your capacity for dealing with them will not feed you positively; rather, they will block your access to happiness.

HAPPINESS MOUNTAIN

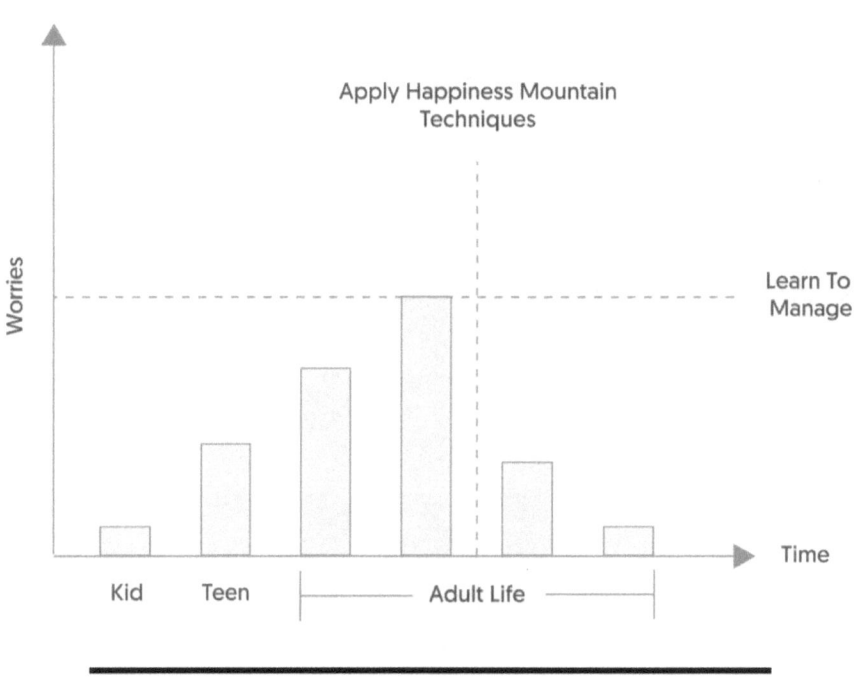

Life with negative-energy management

By climbing Happiness Mountain, you can be happy like a kid again without accumulating worries.

STEP 1: SPOT THE BUG

What is a worry?

A worry is easy to recognize. If you are in thought chains and do not feel good, you worry about something. If you are fully engaged in the activity and happy about it, you are not worrying.

Worry is a response and not the root cause of the unhappy feeling. The Thought Bugs responsible for worries are:

- Anger Thought Bug
- Expectations Thought Bug

- Cravings Thought Bug
- Judgmental Thought Bug
- Fear Thought Bug
- Self-Limiting Thought Bug
- Do-it-Later Thought Bug

All the other Thoughts Bugs cause you to worry.

STEP 2: STOP THE BUG

Power-Up: Mindfulness

Mindfulness Power-Up

Thoughts create worries. They become a problem when you keep dwelling inside your head. Overthinking and not being able to let go are two of the main problems of worrying inside your head. Mindfulness is the opposite of worrying. Mindfulness is living in the present moment and fully engaging in the activity you are currently doing. **The best way to replace the Worry Thought Bug is to walk or do other physical activities to get you out of your head.** The best strategy is to change your scene to get out of your head. Some of the immediate activities you can do mindfully are:

1. Go outside for a walk
2. Take a shower
3. Do moderate to intense exercise
4. Meet a friend
5. Watch a movie to take your mind away from the worry
6. Do an activity connecting with nature
7. Stop thinking until tomorrow. After a good sleep, you will feel better.
8. Use affirmations such as:

- Everything is going to be okay
- I can get through it
- I take it easy
- I will give it some time

When you worry and are stressed, your body produces a hormone called cortisol, and it messages you to act on stress-response activities. You should recognize this and take a break. Do activities mentioned above to help generate serotonin and endorphins, two other types of hormones called Happy Hormones. Serotonin and endorphins will heal your mind and body. You will learn more about stress and how to overcome it with Happy Hormones awareness in Part Four.

STEP 3: ASSESS AND COMPLETE

Sometimes we tend to overthink. Learning to take it easy is the best skill to overcome worry.

ACCEPT AND CREATE

Start with accepting the situation. You can read the Acceptance Power-Up chapter to allow your mind to get started with acceptance. When you accept, your mind gets relaxed. Then you can go deeper to understand what are the next steps.

Accepting the situation makes you ready to create a new future without worrying. Acceptance Power-Up is your best friend to get your positive energy and access the worry with a clear mind.

STOP WORRYING ABOUT THE PAST

There are a million things you can attach to the past. Situations that have happened, such as a breakup of a relationship, the once wonderful life that you had, the money you accumulated that has been depleted, properties you gained and lost, opportunities you didn't take, loved ones you lost, good memories you had in previous jobs. I follow a straightforward principle that I created:

> *Don't worry about things that you cannot take with you when you die.*
>
> — AMAL

Do you take what you worry about with you when you die? Of course not, so you have lost nothing. Those are just experiences you had. You lost nothing since you came into this world with nothing and will leave with nothing.

STOP WORRYING ABOUT THE FUTURE

You worry about the future because you suspect something bad, which creates fear. We will discuss this fear related to worrying under the Fear Thought Bug. For now, separate worry into two parts: past and future.

You might ask, "What about the present?" Usually, if you live in the present, you are actively engaged in day-to-day activities and not worrying. You can only worry about the past or the future. If you think about it, 90 percent of what you worry about is not the actual future. The real future is something you do not know, and you should feel excited to face the unknown rather than be worried.

ADDRESS ROOT-CAUSE BUGS

After calming down by doing the mindfulness activities mentioned above and becoming more aware, you should focus on discovering the root-cause Thought Bug. As I noted, worry is a response and not the root cause. To truly overcome worry, find the root-cause Bugs and address them.

- **Anger Thought Bug:** Are you angry with someone?
- **Expectations Thought Bug:** Have you put an expectation on someone to behave the way you want?
- **Cravings Thought Bug:** Do you have a strong desire? Can you let go or replan in a way that it is aligned to a purpose and not to a strong desire?
- **Judgmental Thought Bug:** Are you not accepting, but judging?
- **Fear Thought Bug:** Are you feeling threatened by future uncertainty?
- **Self-Limiting Thought Bug:** Are your self-limiting thoughts acting on you?
- **Do-it-Later Thought Bug:** Is something you have being procrastinating on making you worried?

Refer to respective Thought Bug chapter to find out how to stop those negative thoughts.

ASK FOR GUIDANCE FROM THE HIGHER POWER

We cannot control everything in the Universe. Sometimes it is good to seek guidance from the higher power when facing challenging times. You can use the following script.

Dear Universe, show me the path to solve [your challenge] and many, many happy years to come.

CHAPTER 18
ANGER THOUGHT BUG

Anger Thought Bug

Anger is a Hard Happiness-Killer. When you are angry, you cannot be happy. When you are angry, you lose your greatness. It will impact your health. Anger is something you need to learn to get over. Life is too short to live in anger.

Let us start with accepting that our default behavior is getting angry when things do not go our way and blaming others. We have to accept anger as an emotion. By knowing how to handle the Anger Bug, you can:

- Minimize the negative response and its impact
- Avoid suffering from anger for long durations
- See clear steps to take
- Quickly move on positively
- Stop living in guilt
- Over time anger starts diminishing from your life
- Able to maintain peace of mind

At times you might get angry. You need to learn to leave it behind and quickly move on. Whatever happened in the past is past. Your Higher Self always leaves the past behind. Guilt is part of the Lower Self. You will learn more about your higher and lower selves in the Inner Happiness section.

STEP 1: SPOT THE BUG

What is Anger?

Anger has different forms. Some are straightforward, and some are not. You will be angry if your energy becomes dark. Whenever you lose your love, forgiveness, kindness, and compassion, there is negative energy created by the Anger Thought Bug. Remember, we are discussing *your* anger, and not the anger of others. On Happiness Mountain, you concentrate on what you have control of.

According to Happiness Mountain, agitation, dislike, hate, bullying, resentment, and annoyance are parts of anger, but you might not recognize them as such. When you are upset with someone, the Anger Bug is hiding in you. Develop the skill to see it. Then it is easy to remove without suffering extended periods of it. Here are some examples:

- You might have a disagreement with your partner about something that matters to you. Both of you become upset and start arguing. You feel like your partner does not understand what you say. And you do not like what your partner says or does. Your energy becomes negative by the words and acts of the other person. Now you have the Anger Bug.
- At work, you could face disagreements. You might feel the other person needs to be corrected or they are unfairly asking things of you. There could be situations other people judge you for and talk about what matters to you in a way you do not like. You may feel upset, and your energy changes to annoyance and dislike. Immediately recognize that your Anger Bug is active.
- You get upset with your children for not doing their schoolwork and spending too much time on their electronic devices. You complain, losing kindness at that moment, and your energy becomes negative.
- While driving, you may see a stranger commit a traffic violation that makes you angry.
- When you go to a restaurant and the speed of service is not what you were expecting, you can get upset and your energy can change to anger.
- One of the service providers is delaying work or not up to your expected standards. You start getting upset, and anger energy flares up.

As you can see, you can radiate negative energy due to anger in any situation. What is the consequence? Angry thoughts drain your energy like holes in a water bucket.

STEP 2: STOP THE BUG

Power-Up: Patience

Patience Power-Up

The most important skill you need to develop is to do nothing until your angry energy is gone. You need to learn to power-up patience. The objective of this step is to stop your negative anger response.

Imagine throwing a pebble in a shallow pond, and ripples form. You must step back and wait until the water has stopped moving for you to see the bottom clearly. You can engage in mindful activities, such as going for a walk or taking a shower.

If the feeling of anger cannot be easily controlled, I recommend using the 24 Hour Pass. Postpone thinking about the matter until after a night's sleep. After a good rest, your waves will calm down and you will be able to understand the issue. Then find the root cause of your anger, which is noted in the following step. Give yourself a pat on the back for not responding to anger!

STEP 3: ASSESS AND COMPLETE

After you calm down, access the situation, looking at how you feel.

Your Feelings	True or false
The situation that occurred is not what you wanted to have happen.	
You feel the other person did not listen to you.	
You are tired and frustrated by the other person's behavior.	
You felt the situation was unfair.	
You feel the other person is not right based on your beliefs.	
An agreement was broken by you or the other party.	

Now think from the other person's perspective and fill in what they would think about the situation and you.

Other person's feelings	True or false
The situation that occurred was not what the other person wanted.	
They feel that I did not listen.	
They are tired and frustrated by my behavior.	
They feel the situation was unfair.	
They feel I am not right based on their beliefs.	
They feel that I judged and said negative things about them.	
An agreement was broken.	

Now that you have a good perspective on the situation, let's look at the Anger Resolution Algorithm. Your intention is to resolve the problem and feel happy.

ANGER RESOLUTION ALGORITHM

The following is a simple but comprehensive plan to eliminate your anger and live a happy life.

- Accept: Take it easy. Time solves everything. Be patient.
- Become aware of your Thought Bugs (you will understand more when reading other Thought Bug chapters).
- Expectation Bug: Are your expectations and the other party's expectations different?
- Judgmental Bug: Did you start judging the other person after you were upset?
- Fear Bug: Is your mind telling a story about a future that has not happened?
- Self-Limiting Bug: Is it a trigger pattern you have from childhood?
- Worry Bug: Are you putting too much significance on the issue?
- Set intentions: Write the positive outcome that you seek.
- Visualize: Picture living with a positive and happy outcome.
- Believe: Know that things are going to be OK.
- Clear away any misunderstandings: Listen and ask questions. Understand why the other party is doing what they are doing. Try to understand the unspoken reason.
- Resolve: Create a positive plan with goals and action for yourself (not for the other party).
- Patience: Calmly and happily give some time to resolve the issue.
- Let go of significance: Surrender the problem and do a physical activity that generates serotonin or endorphins.
- Accept: Affirm any outcome and move on. Be happy that you did what you could do.

You can use the Happiness Mountain app as a tool to make it easy to eliminate the Anger Bug.

APPLY POSITIVE POWER-UPS

Let's start with Positive Power-Ups, which you already learned about in the previous section:

- **Gratitude:** Can you be grateful for something another person has done?
- **Support:** Can you ask the other person how you can help even if you do not like the person right now?
- **Accept:** Can you accept that people are not perfect, and the other person as is, and see their strength rather than weaknesses?
- **Patience:** Are you committed to being patient and not having a negative response to the situation? When your Anger Bug is active, do not try to solve it. Take the Sleepover Pass.
- **Moderation:** Can you be moderate with your views? You do not have to agree with everything the other person says. Agree to disagree, which is acceptance. Let go of your ego and be moderate. Your inner happiness is more important than trying to prove you are right. Let go of the friction. Your life is much bigger than the incident.
- **Love and kindness:** Can you send blessings to better the situation for both of you? Can you be compassionate and look at the other person's views? Can you forgive? Set a new intention for the relationship and drive the matter with purpose. Visualize the outcome from the new intention. After visualizing, your mind and surrounding energies will align with the desired result.
- **Integrity:** Most anger conflicts arise because of misunderstandings. Two parties can have different expectations when there is no understanding. At that moment, communicate and establish an understanding. Then follow through with the agreement with integrity

and authenticity. Sometimes you have to agree to disagree and come to a resolution by letting go of your ego.
- **Mindfulness:** Can you enjoy the life experiences you are already blessed with and take it easy on the other person?

You cannot remember everything when you are mad. If it is a small matter, power-up patience immediately by remembering the picture: stop, smile, and stay calm.

If it is a significant matter, then find this book again and reread this chapter. If you have the app, follow the relevant steps.

CHAPTER 19
EXPECTATION THOUGHT BUG

Expectation Thought Bug

The Expectation Thought Bug is a Silent Happiness-Killer. You may think that putting expectations on others will bring happiness, but they can backfire, and you will be disappointed. The expectation is the number one Thought Bug for causing issues in marriages and love relationships.

STEP 1: SPOT THE BUG

WHAT EXPECTATIONS ARE YOU PUTTING ON OTHERS?

Our human nature makes us put expectations on others, your spouse or partner, children, friends, work colleagues. Most of the time, the leading cause of unhappiness in a relationship is the Expectation Thought Bug. In a marriage or a committed relationship, this is one of the significant culprits of conflict. Whenever you are upset with your children, the most likely reason is your Expectation Thought Bug. Be mindful of spending time with your children, and guide them in the right direction rather than putting your expectations on them. The Expectation Thought Bug could also arise in workplace conflicts. Without properly acknowledging this Bug, you may entirely blame the other person with your Judgmental Bug.

STEP 2: STOP THE BUG

POWER-UP: ACCEPTANCE

Acceptance Power-Up

Replace expectation with acceptance of the person and situation. Take it easy. Do not let your mind create stories. Accept and give time and space to heal. Change your attitude from expectation to love and guidance. **Become an influencer without expectations.**

When things do not go as you expected, your initial response will be anger and you may judge the other person. Let's say you are upset with your partner. Your mind wants to complain, passively or aggressively. You should consciously calm yourself and let the anger subside before moving forward. It would be best to step back from the situation so you can think objectively. Do not cling to the problem.

STEP 3: ASSESS AND COMPLETE

When you are upset with someone, ask yourself if you have put too many expectations on them. Give the situation space, without expecting anything from them. Once you accept the situation, you will have the power to listen to and guide them.

You should let go of your expectations and see how you can help in a conflict you might find yourself in. We are all different souls with our own paths. This applies to your loved ones too. We came alone to this world, and we will leave alone. If it relates to your spouse or partner, children, or parents, think of ways you can give love unconditionally. Be patient. Give space. With children, offer guidance and maintain a state of mindfulness whenever you spend time with them. At work, have clear roles and responsibilities. Let the other person know your expectations up front. If they cannot meet them, look at their strengths and talk to them. Listen to them. The bottom line is to let go of your expectations and focus on giving back through love, guidance, and listening attentively. If you want to be happy, letting go of expectations is a skill you must improve upon.

Neil Pasricha's book *The Happiness Equation* has an excellent technique for letting go of expectations and creating positive outcomes:

AMAL INDI

Want nothing + do everything = have everything.

— NEIL PASRICHA

    Your stress, fear, and anger go away when you do things without expectations. Your free mind has immense positive energy to do things and make a difference. You can apply the Happiness Equation to all your relationships, and they will become great. *The Happiness Equation* is a great book, and I recommend it to everyone.

CHAPTER 20
CRAVING THOUGHT BUG

Craving Thought Bug

The Craving Thought Bug is a Silent Happiness-Killer. We don't only have cravings for food. Any strong desire is a craving in your mind. It could be for alcohol, sex, achievements, or buying things. You might wonder why I noted achievements. When you strongly want to achieve something, there is good side and a stressful side. In order to reach your achievements happily and without stress, you should not make it a strong desire; rather, set an intention and follow a mindful goal-achieving process to reach your achievement.

You may be misled by strong desires, hoping they will bring happiness, but they can bring unhappiness. Cravings can grow into obsessions, addictions, worries, and stress.

STEP 1: SPOT THE BUG

WHAT ARE CRAVINGS?

As human beings, we naturally tend to have desires. This is normal. But strong desires can grow into unhealthy thought patterns, such as:

ADDICTIONS

People can get obsessed with alcohol, casual sex, drugs, porn, games, gambling, etc. These are based on dopamine needs. Refer to the chapter "Feeding Happy Hormones in Unhealthy Ways." These obsessions take your focus away. Power up moderation so you don't become obsessed with these desires. Different people have different types of addiction based Craving Bugs such as:

- Sex Craving Bug
- Drugs Craving Bug
- Alcohol Craving Bug
- Porn Craving Bug
- Food Craving Bug

Start observing your thoughts and identify when the Thought Bug gets activated.

GREED

Greed makes us run the rat race. As humans, we want more and more, be it wealth, power, fame, etc. Be conscious of the greedy behavior of the default human mind. Be grateful for what you have and create more with good intentions.

STRESSFUL STRONG DESIRES TO HAVE OR ACCOMPLISH

Strong desires can bring a craving for any activity. For example, you want to meet a deadline, you want your business to succeed as per your plan, you want to meet sales targets set at the beginning of the year. There are many cases where people act with cravings to achieve sales targets and compromise their well-being and life ethics. Goals are good, but running after goals with cravings is not the right approach, since cravings create negative energy.

STEP 2: STOP THE BUG

POWER-UP: MODERATION

Moderation Power-Up

Replace your intense desire-based cravings with moderation. Step back and give space to think broadly about your life. Establish integrity. I want to highlight that you do not have to fight with strong desires—instead, power up moderation. Step back and get involved in a physical activity.

If you suppress strong desires without shifting to the right state of mind, you may be unable to hold on to the decision. You could use willpower to suppress strong desires. Start with moderation to decide the best approach for you. When you step back with moderation, you will see the best steps to take.

STEP 3: ASSESS AND COMPLETE

Let's address the following life scenarios:

- Addictions
- Greed
- Achieving life goals

ADDICTIONS

Addictions such as drugs, porn, alcohol, casual sex, and workaholism are caused by your mind seeking dopamine-based pleasure. To overcome them, create joy in your life with all four Happy Hormones. When you are addicted, you are not enjoying serotonin and endorphins in healthy forms. Do more nature activities to increase your serotonin levels. Do physical activities to activate your endorphins. You will learn how to create a balanced life in Happiness Experience Three: Living a balanced and joyful life using your Happy Hormones, Dopamine, Oxytocin, Serotonin, and Endorphins. The following are the gradual steps:

- Step back, powering up moderation.
- Increase joy with serotonin, endorphins, oxytocin, and reduce the joy from addition based dopamine.
- Observe your thoughts and stop Thought Bug thoughts immediately. If you spot them, you can stop them.
- Create a higher purpose in life and spend more time on the purpose.
- Stop associating with addicted people.

GREED

Greed is a strong desire to have more. If you are greedy, you will never feel happy. Your mind will keep seeking more and more.

Becoming fulfilled is more important than going after things with greed. Greed is part of your Lower Self. You must connect with your Higher Self and let go of your greed. Aligning with your purpose and setting good intentions will help you to overcome your greed. You will learn more about your Higher Self in Parts 5 and 6, including how to discover your greatness with purpose. Be happy with what you have and create more happily without greed. Daily gratitude will help you to be happy with what you have right now.

ACHIEVING LIFE GOALS

Always drive your life with purpose. Strong desires help when you want to achieve something, but the energy of craving can make you stressed. Achieve life goals without cravings by setting intentions with a higher purpose. Then you can create a series of small steps and follow the step until you reach the goal. Do every step as a happy experience. You will learn goal-achieving with power in Happiness Experience Six: Life Fulfillment with happiness, health, and wealth, doing what you love.

CHAPTER 21
JUDGMENTAL THOUGHT BUG

Judgmental Thought Bug

The Judgmental Thought Bug is a Soft Happiness-Killer, meaning you can't see that you are losing your happiness. Still, you radiate negative energy that impacts your overall happiness. The Judgmental Thought Bug could lead to the Anger

Thought Bug. The Judgmental Thought Bug can take away your greatness as a human being.

STEP 1: SPOT THE BUG

What is negative judging?

Human nature dictates that when expectations are not met or do not align with our beliefs, we start to judge. The default setting of your mind judges and adds meaning to everything you hear or see. You need to recognize this behavior.

Why do you think it is hard to identify the Judgmental Thought Bug? Although it is easy to tell when an individual is judging you, the reverse is not easy to identify. In reality, we judge everything that we see. We add meaning and create stories. We judge race, gender, politics, and religion. You are likely to recognize this behavior within yourself, but there is so much more to the Judgmental Bug than this.

When you are upset with someone, see the following sequence of occurrences:

1. You had an expectation or belief, and the other person did not act according to it.
2. You started judging.
3. Slight anger or negativity was created.

The above is a widespread pattern. It could happen your whole life if you do not recognize it. Let's look at some examples:

- Think about how often you thought negatively about your partner when they did not do what you wanted.
- If you ask a favor from a friend and they fail to perform, your immediate reaction is to get upset and judge them because of their shortcomings.
- Others' opinions on religion, politics, or gender are different from yours.

- When you talk about a friend while that person is not present, you casually judge.
- You judge yourself, which reflects the level of your self-love and confidence.

As a rule of thumb, remember this principle:

> Any time you put a human being down with your thoughts, words, and actions, your Judgmental Thought Bug springs into action.

COMPARISON BUG

Another form of judgment is your comparison with others. This is a sibling of the Judgmental Bug. Our minds tend to compare what we have and what we do not have with others. Jealousy is a result of comparison with others.

STEP 2: STOP THE BUG

Power-Up: Love

Love Power-Up

When you are judging someone, step back and radiate love using your love package.

- Send blessings by wishing them happiness and good health.
- Understand their feelings with empathy.
- Understand their suffering by being compassionate.
- Do an act of kindness.
- Forgive any mistakes.

For example, you could start judging if you get upset with your partner over a disagreement. You begin to see negative things about them. That is the natural default behavior of the mind. At that moment, you can pray and send blessings to understand each other and create a loving and happy situation that is good for both of you.

Then you can do a random act of kindness or ask if there anything you can help with. Be compassionate and understand the other person's points of view. Have empathy toward them, and do not hurt their feelings with your passively or actively aggressive behaviors. Also, through prayer, forgive the other person and yourself for your negative thoughts about them. Your greatness is keeping your mind clean and always creating a positive world around you. If your partner acts negatively, forgive them, knowing they are not at their best at the moment, and stop judging.

At the end of the day, we all try to live happily in this world. At the same time, we are all going through challenges and trying to survive. Our job is not to judge the shortcomings of others, but to give love. We are not perfect, so why would we judge others? Always learn to take it easy with yourself and others.

STEP 3: ASSESS AND COMPLETE

Let's access, understand, and see how to complete, both judgments and comparing negative thoughts.

JUDGMENTS

To overcome the Judgmental Thought Bug, act with your Higher Self by powering up your eight core positive values:
   1. Be **grateful** to the person you tend to judge.
   2. **Raise them up** instead of thinking negatively about them.
   3. **Accept** the other person the way they are.
   4. Be **patient** and stop negative thoughts.
   5. Come to **moderation** and resist judgmental thoughts.
   6. Activate your **love package** and perform an act of **kindness**.
   7. Keep your **integrity** as your greatness, and do not compromise.
   8. Be **mindful** and do not cling to stories inside your head. Focus on the good things you are doing and let go of negative thoughts.

Live in your greatness 100 percent, no matter what. Reprogram your mind to be in your Higher Self, as noted above, and live an extraordinary life.

COMPARISON

One of my good friends introduced me to an excellent technique to overcome Comparison Thought Bug. The technique is wishing good things for others, and uplifting them before your mind starts comparing and creating stories inside your head. Let's look at some examples.

- I see a nice car I do not own. I wish the owner safe and happy travels.
- I go to the lovely house of a friend. I wish my friend prosperity.

- I see someone beautiful. I wish the person happiness and more beauty.
- I see someone rich. I wish them more prosperity and happiness.
- I meet a family with happy kids. I wish them happiness, health, and wealth.
- I see someone successful in their career. I wish them more success and happiness.

When you make a wish, you become part of their happiness, and you become happier. Since you get connected to their vibration, you start attracting similar things to your life. Your mind will not have room for negative comparison thoughts. Wishing others success is an effective technique that you can practice.

CHAPTER 22
FEAR THOUGHT BUG

Fear Thought Bug

F ear can be caused by physical threats or future uncertainty. The negative energy we are discussing here as Fear Thought Bug is only limited to suspicion caused by future uncertainty. Fear caused by suspicion is a Soft Happiness-Killer. Suspicion creates stories in the head. Those stories make you worried. You could lose the energy that you could have used to face challenges when they show up. If you do not identify the Fear Thought Bug, you will lose your happiness and peace. People live with the Fear Thought Bug their whole life, and lose their happiness and well-being.

STEP 1: SPOT THE BUG

WHAT IS FEAR CAUSED BY SUSPICION?

Suspicion is the reason for some of your fear. If a dog comes to bite you right now and you feel fear, that is not suspicion. On the other hand, if you suspect something is likely to happen in the future and become fearful, that is the Suspicion Thought Bug. Let's look at some examples that happened to me in the past:

- Based on some unconfirmed news, I was worried about my job. The problematic event had not happened yet, but my mind was already suffering from fear of job loss. I was worried about how to pay my mortgage.
- I thought my girlfriend was cheating on me, with no facts. I started to feel the Fear and Anger Thought Bugs.
- I started a business and got scared later, thinking it would not work. Even before failing, suspicion was setting me up to fail.
- I was worried and feared that I did not have enough money for retirement.
- I was worried that I could not find a partner. Here, the suspicion was causing the Fear Thought Bug to remove my happiness and confidence.

Understanding fear caused by suspicion helped to make a big difference in my happiness. Now I do not feel fear from suspicion. I may feel fear for a second, but I recognize it as suspicion so I can clear these thoughts immediately. I set an intention and face any future uncertainty with courage.

STEP 2: STOP THE BUG

Power-Up: Gratitude

Gratitude Power-Up

The objective of this step is to immediately get rid of negative energy so that you can handle the situation effectively. When suspicion arises, the mind wants to look for failures and cause you to feel fear. Since you now know the human mind's process, what you can do immediately is to be grateful for what you have. We are blessed to have this life and many things to call our own. Offer gratitude to everyone in your life and everything you possess, as noted in the Gratitude chapter. Gratitude will eliminate the mind's ability to go to the negative side. Another critical point is to trust the universe and ask it, or your higher power, to give you guidance. Once you turn your mind in a positive direction, you can face your life with happiness no matter the situation.

STEP 3: ASSESS AND COMPLETE

With a positive mindset, write out (do not merely think about) all the possible scenarios you're suspicious of. You have two types of outcomes for the suspicion that you need to be aware of. Write down both the possibilities:

1. Positive outcome
2. Negative outcome—fear related to this outcome

You need to write both cases. Let's take the example of job-loss related fear:

Positive outcome:

- You do not lose your job.
- You lose your job and find a new one.
- You apply for other jobs and find a new one before initially losing your job.

Negative outcome:

- You lose your job and do not find a new one for a while.
- You face financial difficulties (write down the specifics).

Now you can clearly see possible scenarios without worrying. If you are processing the outcomes internally, you will most likely see only the negative scenario and feel fear because, as human beings, we are designed for survival. When you are in survival mode, you cannot create. You become depressed, and the probability of your negative scenario occurring increases.

Now that you have clarity on the positive and negative scenarios, there are three things you must do:

PREPARE FOR BOTH POSITIVE AND NEGATIVE SITUATIONS

Instead of worrying, write about whichever outcome you like as an intention. The best time to do this is early in the morning when your mind is free of clutter. When you set the intention, you start to see the actions you should take.

Set up an **action plan for both positive and negative situations** that can occur. You cannot solve everything in a negative situation. You have to believe that things are going to be OK and focus on the positive action plan.

REPEAT POSITIVE AFFIRMATIONS

Your mind will take you to the negative aspect of a situation and scare you unless you have some positive affirmations. Before you go to sleep, or right when you wake up, say your positive affirmation list. A few affirmations that I read are:

- I am smart enough and intelligent enough to achieve anything I want.
- I am attracting more and more abundance simply by being the great person I am.
- [Affirmation for your fear converted to positive outcome].

ASK FOR GUIDANCE FROM THE HIGHER POWER

Trust the Universe or God and ask for guidance in the following format:

> "Dear God, please show me the path to [positive outcome you desire] and many, many years to come."

Preparation for positive and negative outcomes, daily affirmations, and seeking guidance from a higher power will help you to overcome your Fear Thought Bug.

CHAPTER 23
SELF-LIMITING THOUGHT BUG

Self-Limiting Thought Bug

The Self-Limiting Thought Bug is a Soft Happiness-Killer. The root cause of the Self-Limiting Bug is your self-limiting beliefs. This is hard to identify, and you could suffer with them your whole life. Self-limiting beliefs are caused by old programs created in your subconscious mind by trauma during your childhood and beyond. It will help if you put effort into identifying the Self-Limiting Bug. Please note that this is not medical advice. I am sharing how I overcame my own self-limiting beliefs.

STEP 1: SPOT THE BUG

What is a self-limiting belief?

You were born into this world with an empty and clean mind. Little by little, your mind got programmed. You absorbed meanings from what you saw, felt, and heard. You started to recognize your parents. You began to identify home. You got a nice name, and you began to respond when someone called you by it. You built your character from experiences during childhood. Some were good ones, helping your happiness and success. Some were not-so-good ones, distracting you from happiness and success. Some of the not not-so-good ones caused trauma with the following characteristics:

- You went through an intense emotional experience and it registered in your subconscious. For example: trauma caused by your parents' divorce, getting bullied at school, losing a loved one during childhood, seeing substance abuse by your parents, not getting enough love at home, childhood incidents with siblings.
- You still remember those traumatic experiences.
- You created a self-limiting character pattern without your knowledge.
- As an adult, you use this self-limiting pattern of behavior without knowing it.

Trauma has happened to most of us. That is OK. The mind picks up cues from its childhood environment. The problem is not the trauma. The problem is that not everyone identifies and cleanses them, which all adults can do. I believe everyone *must* do a trauma-cleansing process. I thought that I had a good childhood, without trauma. Then I realized I had experienced a lot of trauma, such as getting bullied at school and many others examples. I did the cleansing, and I am so glad I did. If you have not already cleansed old programs, it is time to recognize and get rid of them so that you can have a happy and successful life. We call these weak programs Self-Limiting Thought Bugs, because they limit your happiness. You are unique, and you have greatness. One of the main barriers to your greatness is your Self-limiting Thought Bug.

You can identify your behavior patterns caused by the Self-Limiting Bug by closely looking at your self-talk. The following are common self-limiting beliefs:

- I am not good enough
- Nobody loves me
- I am alone
- I can't be my real self or I'll be judged
- I am not smart enough
- I do not know enough
- I do not have enough money
- My work is not appreciated
- I do not belong
- Nobody listens to me
- I am small
- I am too old
- I am not pretty enough
- I am not educated enough

This way of thinking stays for a lifetime unless you reprogram yourself to get rid of these beliefs. It is essential to be aware of this, because they impact your love relationships, career, social relationships, and everything else in your life. This is one of the biggest barriers for adults to becoming happy.

If you want to know more details, I recommend following Dr. Joe Dispenza. He is a famous neuroscientist and author. You can listen to him on YouTube. An excellent book to read is his *Breaking the Habit of Being Yourself: How to Lose Your Mind and Create a New One*.

Let me share an example from my life. In my family, I am the youngest of four siblings. I have two brothers and one sister. When my brothers and sister graduated high school with good grades and attended university, everyone was happy and celebrated. By the time I graduated with good grades and attended university, it had become the norm in our family. When I got my high school results, they weren't much of a surprise, and I was not appreciated for what I had done. When my brother got admitted to medical school, it was a celebratory matter for the family. When I went to the engineering university, I felt it was not appropriately celebrated. I thought nobody cared about my achievements, and nobody loved me.

The beliefs became:

- Nobody cares about me, so in my relationships I sought a lot of attention.
- Nobody appreciated my work, so I got upset in the absence of appreciation. This was made more apparent if I did something good, but the gesture was not reciprocated.

As you can see, these programmed behaviors contributed to the failure of my relationships and my inability to have a successful life. This is a potential of how self-limiting beliefs can truly affect an individual. Most people live their whole lives without noticing the destructive, programmed child inside them. They can never love someone fully since the Thought Bugs take away their power.

STEP 2: STOP THE BUG

Power-Up: Uplift

Uplift Power-Up

Positive affirmations and positive thinking raise your self-esteem. Create a list of positive affirmations, such as:

- I am happy and grateful now that everyone loves me.
- I am grateful now that I am awesome, and I do not need attention, appreciation, acceptance, and approval from others to be happy.
- I am smart and intelligent enough to achieve anything I want.
- I am a loving and kind person who makes a positive impact in the world.

I have seen many people using positive affirmations without seeing results and becoming disappointed. Positive affirmations are good, but they will not fully resolve the long-hidden childhood trauma-driven self-limiting beliefs.

STEP 3: ASSESS AND COMPLETE

The following is the process that I followed to cleanse my self-limiting beliefs:

- **List trauma:** Identify your childhood trauma events and the associated self-limiting beliefs.
- **Adult behaviors:** Identify your adult behaviors and triggers associated with your self-limiting beliefs.
- **Positive affirmations:** Develop positive affirmations to overcome self-limiting beliefs.
- **Counter experiences:** Create new and happy counter-experiences for self-limiting beliefs and invalidate them with self-confidence.
- **Higher consciousness:** Stay in your higher consciousness with Happiness Power-Ups to maintain your self-confidence and prevent the Self-Limiting Bug from acting on you.

I will take you through some examples from my life to make it simple to understand. You can follow the process while reading by downloading a worksheet from
happinessmountain.com/book/resources

STEP 1: LIST TRAUMA

Let's first understand what trauma is, according to the Cambridge Dictionary:

Trauma *n.*
Severe and lasting emotional shock and pain caused by an extremely upsetting experience or a case of such shock happening:
The trauma of marriage breakdown

He had psychotherapy to help him deal with his childhood traumas.[1]

The first step to recovery is knowing what your trauma is. You do not forget trauma because it was an intense experience for you. Think about what you remember as a child from age three to twelve years. You do not remember everything, but you remember some things. Now analyze what you remember and see the self-limiting patterns you created from them.

Let's complete your list. Write every incident you remember from age three to twelve. They must be specific events in your life. Early-age incidents have the highest impact, and most of the programs were already created by the time you reached your teenage years. Although specific high-impact incidents can happen at any point while you are growing up, I am simply sharing my experiences and how I overcame them. Here are few examples:

STEP 2: IDENTIFY ADULT BEHAVIORS

Now think of your current behaviors. When do you get triggered the most? Here are some examples of my behaviors before reprogramming:

Self-Limiting Belief	Trigger Points
I do not belong	I do not connect with other people in group settings.
I am being judged	I do not share my opinions in group settings.
I am not loved	I look for love all the time, to the level that I annoy my partner and invade her space. When I do not feel loved, I get upset, which creates an unhappy environment for everyone I am surrounded by.
I am unworthy	I try to stay low-key, and I am unable to be myself comfortably with other people.
Nobody cares what I do or achieve	If someone does not appreciate good work, I get upset.

STEP 3: POSITIVE AFFIRMATIONS

The first step toward reprogramming the mind to overcome low self-esteem programs is to build a good set of affirmations and repeat them at night or in the morning:

- I am always protected and loved by the higher power.
- I always live in my Higher Self, positively impacting the world.
- I am blessed to have this awesome life.
- Everyone loves me, and I love everyone.
- I am smart and intelligent enough to achieve anything I want.
- I am here to help and serve others and make a difference.
- I live an abundant life with happiness, health, and wealth.

STEP 4: CREATE COUNTER-EXPERIENCES

The next step to reprogramming the mind is to create happy experiences that invalidate old beliefs. These new experiences will go to your body's memory and start to invalidate old experiences. Following are a few examples of how to reprogram the mind out of the old beliefs.

I am not loved:

- Believe that the higher power always loves me and guides my journey.
- Build good relationships with loved ones and be of service to others.
- Make real connections with people.
- Stay connected with nature and the higher power every day.

I am being judged

- Life is too short to be bothered by what others think.
- Be myself and love myself.
- Share my opinion in meetings and consciously not worry about being judged.
- Think about the impact, not about the self.
- Don't overthink.

I do not belong

- Actively participate in group settings.
- Make real connections with people.
- Help others to achieve what they want.

I am unworthy

- I love my life and myself.
- I always live in my Higher Self no matter what.
- I highly value myself, my work, and my time.
- I say no, and I do not have to please everyone.
- I live with integrity and honor.

Nobody cares what I do or achieve.

- Let go of expectations and be in service.
- Be happy for others' success.
- Make a positive impact without expectations and look for appreciation.

STEP 5: HIGHER CONSCIOUSNESS

Maintaining a higher consciousness is essential to be able to see your thoughts and alter your behaviors. It is also necessary to stay away from alcohol and drugs, which impact your consciousness. The key to higher consciousness is embedding the eight Positive Power-Ups into your value system and living accordingly.

Overcoming the Self-Limiting Bug is the best gift you can give yourself. You will feel free from the shackles of your own self-limiting beliefs, which will create a happier way of living. Circumstances do not trigger me. I feel blessed to be able to recognize and defeat them. Now I am at peace and happy.

What you say and feel is what you attract in life. This is called the "law of attraction." You will learn more about it in the Happiness Experience Six. Let's get the foundation right so that you climb to the higher levels of Happiness Mountain faster.

As you already know, I was not born with positive programming, but I reprogrammed myself for what I wanted. If I could reprogram myself, despite all the things I started with, you can too. You should spend time reflecting on the Self-limiting Thought Bug. Be specific and remember your childhood events clearly so you can truly identify past traumas and make sure they do not affect you anymore. Please don't waste this wonderful human life because of old self-limiting programs in your subconscious. Invest time in getting over your self-limiting beliefs. Be free from them. I feel free, and I believe this is one of the greatest forms of happiness one can have. Please do not miss it.

CHAPTER 24

DO-IT-LATER THOUGHT BUG

Procrastination Thought Bug

The Do-it-Later Thought Bug causes you to procrastinate. It is a Soft Happiness-Killer. You cannot increase your happiness when you have a long list of unhandled tasks. You get more energy when you handle them because the negative energy lingering in your mind is no more. Therefore, it is essential to understand your Do-it-Later Thought Bug.

STEP 1: SPOT THE BUG

What is procrastination?

Procrastination is easy to recognize. Think about some actions or task lingering in your head that you want to do but have not done. You might find some of them staying for a long time if you don't take action. Now categorize and prioritize them. Procrastination is not always bad. Procrastination applies to two types of categories:

- If you do not complete something that is simple, then you are procrastinating. When you pile up day-to-day activities, your stress level goes up at the end. Therefore, it is vital to clear out tasks on the list to keep your mind happy. Take action now when your mind says to do it later.
- There are certain cases where you are still collecting information and processing it before taking action. By delaying taking action, particularly in creative work, you obtain more data, resulting in more ideas and opportunities to put them together.
- There are bigger life goals that require you to break them into smaller pieces and accomplish them.

STEP 2: STOP THE BUG

Power-Up: Integrity

Integrity Power-Up

Establishing integrity is the solution to procrastination. The first thing to start with is understanding what you need to do and prioritizing tasks in life. Write down what you are procrastinating on. Accept the fact that you cannot finish everything and be perfect. You can use the three-D strategy:

- **Do not do:** See what you can eliminate. Your time is essential. What are the day-to-day tasks you are going to do? Is it needed? Learn to say no to people based on your priorities.
- **Delegate:** See which tasks you can delegate. You do not have to do everything by yourself. Get support. For example, you can get professional cleaners to clean your house thoroughly once a month.
- **Do it by yourself:** Follow the step 3 below.

STEP 3: ASSESS AND COMPLETE

The short- and long-term solution for procrastination is integrity. If it is a simple task that you know how to do, you should just do it. If it is a complex task, think about it from an integrity point of view and complete it. Ask the question, "Is it suitable for my integrity not to do the particular task?" You will see the answers and acquire the energy to complete the task. Have integrity for yourself to complete things for your own sanity.

Have a schedule and follow it with integrity. This helps to stop wasting time on impromptu tasks. Every morning, I add my Happiness Schedule to the Happiness Mountain app. Convert tasks to happiness experiences and complete them.

Another skill you need is focus. You should be able to keep your mind on one thing until the end. Use meditation as your training, which will help you focus. Do ten minutes daily of meditation using the Happiness Mountain app. You can also use more specialized meditation apps.

SELF-MOTIVATION

If you feel stressed or dislike doing something, you need motivation to complete the task. To get motivation, you can imagine the benefits you get after completing the task. This will give you the dopamine to finish it.

Five steps for self-motivation:

- Start with the **intention.**
- **Visualize** the outcome.
- **Visualize** the doing the task as a happy experience.
- **Do** the task as a happy experience.
- **Celebrate** when you finish.

HOW DO YOU EAT AN ELEPHANT?

If you want to conquer an extensive and time-consuming task or goal, the best approach is to break it into smaller steps or tasks and complete one step at a time. The mind loves to overthink and get overwhelmed by the job or the goal. Consciously identify the nature of the mind and get used to framing your mind to think only about the minor step and accomplish it. When you complete one step, you get dopamine from that accomplishment, which motivates you to do the next step.

THE 5 MINUTE RULE

> If you don't want to do something, make a deal with yourself to do at least five minutes of it. After five minutes, you'll end up doing the whole thing.
>
> — KEVIN SYSTROM, INSTAGRAM FOUNDER

Our mind does not like to do things that it feels like it is not enjoying. To get around that is the five-minute rule where you commit to do it for five minutes. Framing the mind only for five minutes will help you to get started. Once you get started, you will likely accomplish what you want to achieve. Train your mind to follow this rule to overcome procrastination substantially.

TIME DIARY

If you wish to have high efficiency and overcome procrastination, use a time diary. Every time you start something, record the time it started. When you end it, record the finish time. In between, you should not do multitasking. Give your 100% mindfulness to the task you are doing. If you need a break, record it in the time diary. Throughout the day, record your activities. Then you can see what time you are spending. You will catch the unproductive times, such as if you are on social media or talking around. I use this technique when I want to be highly productive. It would help if you did at least for a week to improve yourself. Time Diary is especially important when you are at a time when you want to achieve a goal. This technique helps you to become mindful and conscious of your time usage. Make sure to take a break at the end of the day and let go and relax or do an activity that generates endorphins.

Happiness Experience Three: Living a Joyful and Balanced Life

CHAPTER 25

FOUR HAPPY HORMONES: DAILY DOSE

Happy Hormones are the second-best thing I mastered to become happy. Negative Thought Bugs were the first things I mastered, because I realized that with negative thoughts lingering in my head, I could never have a happy life. As crucial as removing negativity is, learning to be joyful is also essential. Most people understand happiness as feelings of joy, the ones you get from Happy Hormones. And there are only four Happy Hormones for you to know to make your life consciously joyful. Happy Hormones are also called "feel-good hormones."

For example, you can go out to drink with friends and be happy. What happens within you is that your body triggers two types of Happy Hormones, oxytocin, and dopamine, which make you feel joy as follows:

- Being with friends means you feel love, bonds, and trust, so your body produces oxytocin, which translates to feeling joy.

- Drinking alcohol responsibly gives you pleasure, and your body produces dopamine. You feel joy with that experience.

Another example is having a dog. You have heard the saying that a dog is man's best friend. Dogs bond with their owners and the owner produces oxytocin, making them happy.

Happiness is a mind and body function. Once you understand Happy Hormones, you can consciously design your activities so that you produce them in every activity. Make activities experiences that make up your joyful day.

HUMAN HAPPINESS DESIGN IS THE SAME FOR EVERYONE

Another critical point is that Happy Hormones are common to people worldwide, irrespective of what country or culture you belong to. Nevertheless, what you do to trigger Happy Hormones could differ based on your environment and culture. The fundamentals of happiness are common to everyone in this world. For example, you become happier when you meet a friend you love. It is common for any person in the world. Each of us has different friends, and the fundamentals of happiness are the same. Another typical example is having a dog. Irrespective of culture and country, having a dog with love and bond makes humans happy.

FUNDAMENTALS OF HUMAN HAPPINESS

I went to school for thirteen years of my life. I went to university for another four years and completed a degree. I did all the steps to get a good job and be happy—yet I did not study enough about Happy Hormones and how they can help day-to-day to design a joyful life. A solid understanding of Happy Hormones is the key to a happy and healthy life. With this knowledge, you can improve your relationships, work situation, and health, and everything else in your life.

HAPPINESS MOUNTAIN

Joy in life comes as a result of your daily DOSE of Happy Hormones:

1. **D**opamine: drive, motivation, and pleasure
2. **O**xytocin: bonding, trust, and love
3. **S**erotonin: elevated mood and self-esteem
4. **E**ndorphins: healing and well-being

It is essential to enjoy all four types of Happy Hormones to become joyful in a balanced manner. For example, if you focus only on one area, like a dopamine-based workaholic life, your life feels joyful but you are not balanced, and you cannot experience life to the fullest.

HOW TO APPLY THE DOSE

Allow me to share one of my happy daily-life templates so you can understand how I apply this awareness. Like any other successful person I have a schedule for each day, but I call mine a "Happiness Schedule," not a task or meeting list. That is a distinction you should make as a Happiness Mountain climber.

5:00–5:30 a.m.: Morning routine

My wake-up routine is drinking a glass of warm water, light yoga, walking outside the house, feeling the morning freshness, and spending a quiet moment with nature around me. These will give me serotonin and put me in a good mood. I read my affirmations and visualize the life I want to create with Happiness Schedule. Then I get ready with a few goals for the day. Affirmations and daily goals provide the drive for the day by activating dopamine in my system. I get inspired about my day ahead.

. . .

5:30–7:00 a.m.: Creative time

I am an author. I write. I love writing. Before sitting down to write, I do ten minutes of meditation. Meditation and mindfully writing enhance the mood through the release of serotonin and endorphins.

7:00–8:00 a.m.: Connect with nature

Nature is the best healer for the mind and body. I do physical activity as much as possible, connecting with nature. I love outdoor walking or jogging. When I walk, I do not think about other things but connect with nature by simply being present. In winter, I go to the sauna or for an indoor swim. Water is part of nature, and if I do not have time to go out, I take a mindful bath. Doing all my nature activities mindfully releases serotonin, and my mood gets boosted. Activities like going to the gym or sauna or running outdoors create endorphins with lots of sweating to cleanse my body.

8:00–9:00 a.m.: Kids' breakfast and getting ready for school

This is my time for serving my family. I make a nice breakfast with love for the kids and ensure they get ready to go to school on time. This activity involves people, meaning I enjoy oxytocin with love and bonding.

9:00–5:00 p.m.: Work time

This is all about other people and accomplishing company goals. People come first for me. Nurturing good relationships and having a cheerful time with people gives me lots of oxytocin. Then I talk about business matters with a clear and happy mind, with goals for each meeting resulting in dopamine-based joy.

. . .

Apply To Your Life

Your life is different from mine, and Happy Hormones are common for both of us. You may have a busy schedule, traveling to the office, taking care of young children, extended office hours, etc. It is essential to wake up early and have your own time to create positive energy in the morning, which will help with your mood for the day by activating serotonin.

If you have a long drive to your workplace, make that a happy experience by adding something you like: listening to a podcast or music, talking to people, enjoying a coffee, or just observing the beauty of nature.

- Listening to music gives you a good mood through the release of serotonin
- Listening to motivational podcasts gives you drive through dopamine
- Enjoying coffee gives pleasure through dopamine
- Talking to people gives you oxytocin-based joy
- Observing nature with mindfulness brings on a good mood through serotonin

Whatever life you have, you can apply Happy Hormone awareness to create joy in it.

CHAPTER 26

HOW TO CREATE A JOYFUL & BALANCED LIFE

Hormones are your body's chemical messengers. Once released by glands into your bloodstream, they act on various organs and tissues to control everything from the way your body functions to how you feel.

One group of hormones are nicknamed the "feel-good hormones" because of the happy and, sometimes, euphoric feelings they produce. They're also considered neurotransmitters, which means they carry messages across the spaces between nerve cells. What are the four feel-good hormones? Dopamine, serotonin, endorphins, and oxytocin.[1]

NEUROTRANSMITTERS

Imagine a printer at home, and you want to print a document from your computer. How does the printer know what to print? Your computer sends a message to the printer. It could be through Wi-Fi or cable.

Now imagine your body. You have many organs in your body. They are made from different types of cells. You have many communication pathways within the brain and throughout the body. You have a messaging system to communicate from your brain to your different organs, called the central nervous system.

The brain controls how we think, learn, move, and feel. Your body, which consists of organs, needs messages from the brain. Neurotransmitters transmit these messages. Neurotransmitters are generated in parts of the brain called *glands*. Your spinal cord is part of your nervous system, which carries these messages to different parts of your body's organs. One type of these messages we are focusing on here is the message to feel good or happy, called Happy Hormones. Happy Hormones are considered neurotransmitters because they transmit messages to organs. Each Happy Hormone carries different types of body chemicals as feel-good messages from the brain. For example, if your body receives messages consisting of motivation, your body happily moves to accomplish goals.

The following is the four Happy Hormones, a.k.a. neurotransmitters, and the types of messages they transmit to cells:

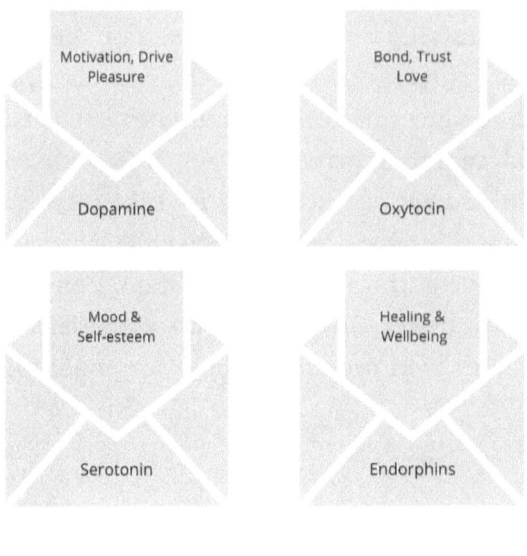

Four Happy Hormones

HOW TO CREATE JOY IN DAILY LIFE ACTIVITIES

Happiness Mountain's approach to Happy Hormones is reverse-engineered. You focus the four types of **feel-good messages as intentions for daily activities** and allow the body to generate the relevant Happy Hormones. For a balanced life, you require all four Happy Hormones. When the body produces the Happy Hormones, you feel good and the activity becomes a joyful experience.

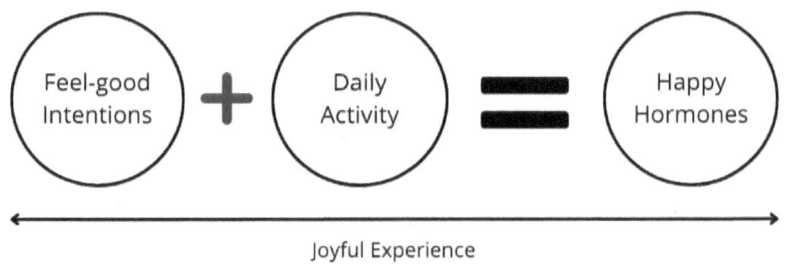

Joyful Experience

FEEL-GOOD INTENTIONS

In Happiness Mountain, we use the power of the mind through intentions to create joyful experiences. The brain is a primary physical component of your mind. The mind goes beyond the physical dimensions and cannot precisely define it. Your human mind is powerful. When you set an intention, it seeks ways to realize the results. Your intentions have energy powered by your life energy. Your intentions have authority over your brain. Consider intentions as messages to your brain. When you do the activities with feel-good intentions, the brain will produce Happy Hormones with the right activity.

Feel-Good Intentions	Happy Hormone (DOSE)
Motivation, drive, and pleasure	Dopamine
Bond, trust, love	Oxytocin
Boost mood and self-esteem	Serotonin
Healing and wellbeing	Endorphins

Happy Hormones are biological parts of the body that you cannot measure by yourself. The way to measure Happy Hormones indirectly is by using your awareness of whether you felt the desired feel-good results. If you feel good, your body has generated the Happy Hormones. For example, you should feel joy if you meet a friend with the feel-good intention of bonding, trust, or love. That means your body triggered oxytocin, and you got the desired result: joy. If you did not feel joy after meeting a friend, you have to reflect and see whether you made a real connection with bonds, trust, or love. You may have a Judgmental Thought Bug preventing the brain from sending feel-good messages to your body. Since you have a higher level of awareness, you can take the corrective actions to build an authentic connection by addressing the Judgmental Bug.

Here, we focus on the feel-good intentions with daily activities, using Happy Hormones as a guiding principle. How you test our results is using your awareness. If you get the desired feel-good results, you have achieved what you wanted: a joyful experience. Since we are not testing the body's Happy Hormones, we assume the relevant Happy Hormones have facilitated the joy.

DAILY ACTIVITIES

Happiness Mountain defines your daily life with six activity types that help you generate Happy Hormones:

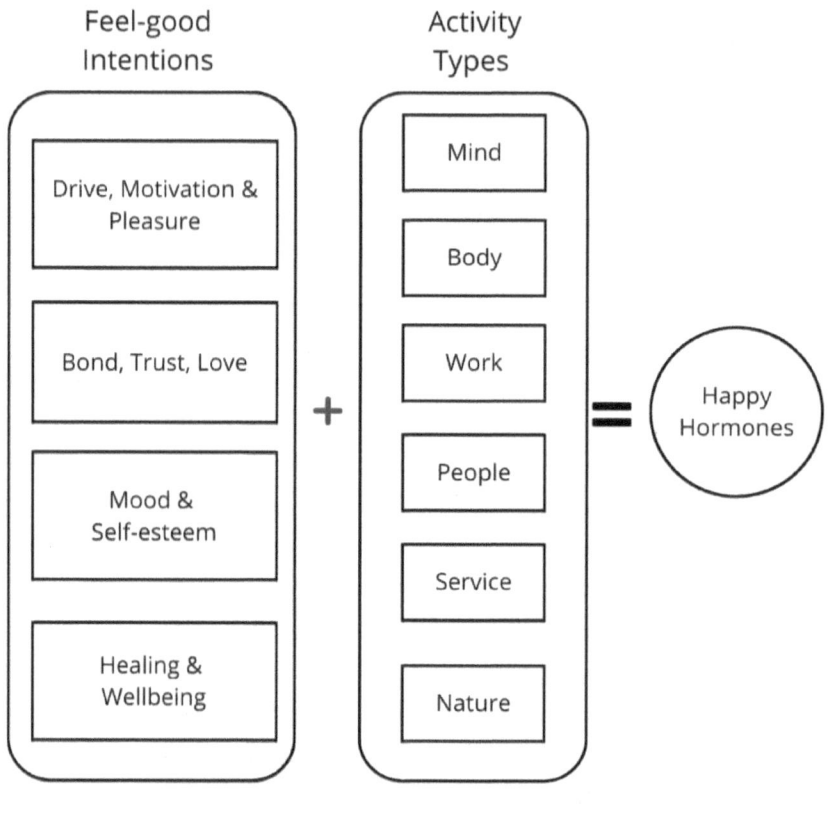

How to Trigger Happy Hormones

There are many ways to categorize your daily activities. I recommend aligning to this categorization if you follow the Happiness Mountain methodology. The Happiness Mountain app will help you to track your daily activities using these categories to boost your energy and become happier. If you don't have the app, use a journal. Tracking is essential while reprogramming your mind to bring your consciousness to creating a balanced life.

- **Mind**: Activities that create a relaxed and positive mind include meditation, prayer, reading a book, affirmations, calming music, doing nothing, taking it easy, listening to mentors, and living mindfully.
- **Body**: Activities relating to health and fitness include exercise, yoga, walking, swimming, sports, intermittent fasting, sauna, eating healthy, and drinking the required amount of water.
- **Work**: Activities relating to work accomplishments.
- **People**: Activities relating to making healthy relationships. Make real connections with others. Make every human interaction happy, including time with family and coworkers and talking to friends or strangers.
- **Service**: Activities relating to service to others and self. For example, I am in service when I make dinner for my family.
- **Nature**: Activities relating to connecting with nature to heal mind and body. Ensure you do at least one activity daily that connects you with nature, such as walking outdoors, observing nature, taking a mindful bath, swimming, hiking, enjoying the sunshine, and doing garden work.

You can create joy in daily life by learning to do daily activities with **relevant feel-good intentions.** For example, you are going to meet a friend.

- Activity type: People

- Feel-good intention: Make a real connection with bonding, trust, and love
- Activity: Meet your friend

When you go with the right intention and act accordingly, your body produces Happy Hormones such as oxytocin, and your experience becomes joyful. You can have more than one type of feel-good intention. For example, if I meet my friend to accomplish something related to work:

- Activity type: Work
- Feel-good intention: Motivation, drive, pleasure
- Activity: Complete reviewing of Part 4 of the book

Activities generate more than one Happy Hormone in the body. You can focus a primary feel-good intention as the driving one to keep it simple and let the body do its magic with the relevant Happy Hormones.

BALANCED LIFE

I was a work-life balance team lead in an organization I used to work for. We did not have a clue what work-life balance meant, because we had no practical definition. We organized some outdoor activities and encouraged everyone to finish work on time and go home as our primary focus for work-life balance. Once I studied the mind, I realized what effective life balance means. Happiness Mountain's definition of a balanced life comes from the balance of Happy Hormones and daily activities.

Your day is balanced when you consciously complete all six types of daily activities and gain all four Happy Hormones' feel-good results.

HAPPINESS MOUNTAIN

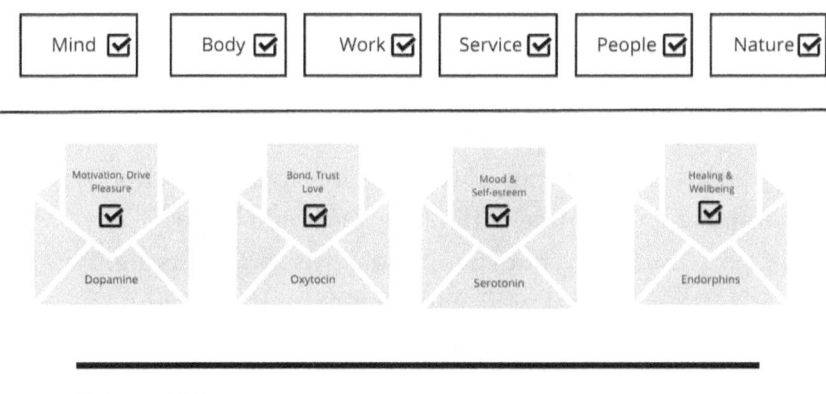

Balanced Life

UNBALANCED LIFE

An unbalanced life is when someone does not consciously complete all six activities and does not gain the four Happy Hormones during the day.

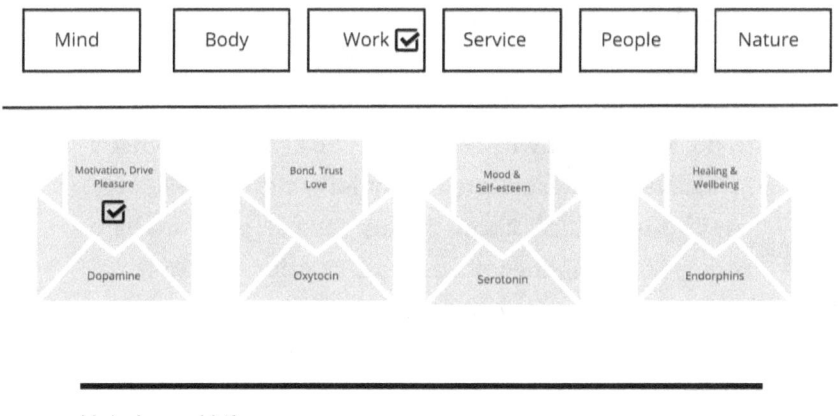

Unbalanced Life

I will explain this with an example. Let's say you are attached to your work and do not have time to take care of your mind and body. You are also very much work-oriented and have no time to care about other people's feelings when you engage with people. In this scenario, you get happiness from dopamine and lack other hormones necessary for a joyful and healthy life.

- You may not have mindful time to spend with your family. You take care of their responsibilities but don't spend quality time with them. You could be physically with the family, but your mind may still be working. You feel important at work and want to fulfill work and family responsibilities. But you are missing oxytocin from spending quality time with your family.
- You get things done but don't make real connections with people at work. You miss the dopamine and related bonding, trust, and love with your work colleagues.
- You are not spending peaceful time keeping your mind calm and happy. You do not have time to go outside and connect with nature. You are always busy thinking about work. You lack the peace and calmness generated from serotonin. You have a high chance of acquiring stress and other health issues.
- You want to go to the gym but often miss it. You feel like exercise is not something you enjoy, but a chore you have to do. You do not work out until you sweat. Your heart rate never increases. You do not have time to take care of your body or don't know the joy you can get from being active. You miss the joy endorphins offer and their benefits for a healthy heart and body.

LIFE FULFILLMENT

You must be balanced to feel life fulfillment. The key is understanding the four Happy Hormones and slowly adding activities to your life. For example, add a daily walk with your family (or dog, if you have one) to produce serotonin and oxytocin. Register for a weekly fitness class, bringing your heart rate to higher levels and sweating. A runner's high will give you endorphins. Join a yoga class to feel calm and release serotonin. Start meditating ten minutes a day. By adding a few of these activities, you receive the benefits of all four Happy Hormones. Once you start enjoying the joy out of all four Happy Hormones, you will feel a different level of joy in life.

HOW TO OVERCOME STRESS

There is another hormone called cortisol which is generated when you are stressed. That is also a neurotransmitter that sends messages to your body to alter behavior to cope with stress. One of the behaviors could be stress-eating to produce dopamine. Another behavior could be forcing yourself to stop working and take a break to produce serotonin.

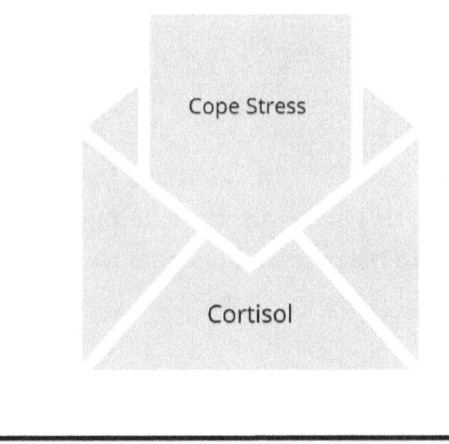

Stress Hormone

If you do not produce enough Happy Hormones or live a balanced life, you may have to deal with stress hormones. If you are stressed, your body will alter your behavior, encouraging you to get feel-good Happy Hormones. At that moment, listen to your body and do Happy Hormone–generating activities such as an outdoor walk. With the outdoor walk, you can produce serotonin and feel relaxed. If you have serotonin, you will be less likely to get stressed and release cortisol.

- **Activity type:** Mind
- **Feel-good intention:** Mood and self-esteem
- **Activity:** Go for a walk outdoors and connect with nature

If you want to relieve the pain from stressful feelings, endorphin-generating activity like moderate to intense exercise will help you to heal you completely.

- **Activity type:** Body
- **Feel-good intention:** Healing and Well-being
- **Activity:** Feel runner's high by intense or lengthy exercise

The stress hormone is helpful in a small amount to alter our stressful behaviors during our busy lives. If you are not producing enough Happy Hormones and are under consistent stress and producing higher amounts of cortisol, it can impact your health and overall happiness. In this scenario, start doing all six types of daily activities to create life balance and address Negative Thought Bugs causing stress.

MAKE EVERY EXPERIENCE A HAPPY EXPERIENCE.

The secret to making every daily activity a happy experience is producing one or more Happy Hormones during the activity. Adding Happy Hormones to your daily activities is like adding salt and pepper to a meal to make it tasty. When the body has one or more Happy Hormones, your experience becomes joyful. You are truly happy inside and out if you do daily activities joyfully. Adding balance lets you live a fulfilling life with happiness and good health.

QUIZ

1. If you want to get motivated to do something, what are the feel-good intentions and the related Happy Hormone you have to focus on?
2. If you want to feel like you need love and bonding, what are the feel-good intentions and related Happy Hormone you have to focus on?
3. If you want to boost your mood, what are the feel-good intentions and related Happy Hormone you have to focus on?
4. If you feel overwhelmed or stressed, what are the feel-good intentions and related Happy Hormones you have to focus on?

In the following four chapters, you can learn more about each Happy Hormone so that you understand **picking activities** for different Happy Hormones in day-to-day life.

CHAPTER 27
DOPAMINE = MOTIVATION + DRIVE + PLEASURE

Feel-good intention	Primary techniques
Motivation, drive, and pleasure	**Motivation**: Set intentions, goals & visualize **Drive**: Take actions as happy experiences **Pleasure**: Celebrate rewards

Dopamine is the key Happy Hormone that makes you feel alive throughout the day. You feel alive when you have desires and work towards them. These are the key areas that dopamine drives:

- To accomplish life goals
- Feel energetic during daily activities
- Pleasure activities like food, sex, games, alcohol, etc.

LIFE IS A JOURNEY, NOT A DESTINATION

When you go on a journey, there are three important stages:

- Initial thoughts and setting the intention to go on the journey
- The experience of going in the journey
- The reward; accomplishment by reaching the destination.

If you are happy during your day-to-day activities, you enjoy life as a journey. On the other hand, if you are waiting for the final reward at the end of the journey, you could work hard but lack daily happiness. Focus on joy along the way toward the final goal. Some people go after end goals and wait to achieve them to become happy. For example, you can work very hard to earn money, have security for your retirement, and not enjoy the individual days of your life.

Another example is working hard to teach your children and send them to college but ignoring your well-being. Or working on a project and becoming stressed. These are examples of your drive to get the reward at the journey's end. The most powerful way to have daily happiness is to start enjoying your life's journey as a series of experiences. By doing that, irrespective of what the result is, you will be happy. Consider the reward at the end as your bonus. Happy people have a higher chance of accomplishing the result.

THREE STEPS TO CONSCIOUSLY TRIGGER DOPAMINE

You get motivated when you think about the reward. Set the default reward as making every experience a happy experience. The mere thought of making an experience happy, triggers your mind to produce dopamine and alters your attitude to be positive. You can have a pleasurable experience by having a positive attitude towards the actions that you need to be taken. If you have a negative attitude toward it, you can produce the stress hormone cortisol and make the activity harder. Therefore, set the intentions for any activity you are doing as follows:

1. **Intention:** Enjoy setting your intention and visualize your ideal results. You just created dopamine, motivation, and drive.
2. **Action:** Have fun listing your action steps. Make each action step a happy experience by taking every step with a positive attitude, resulting in further dopamine, motivation, and drive to continue.
3. **Reward:** When you have achieved your desired results, you will feel happier. Your dopamine levels will skyrocket. Celebrate for even more!

Intention, action, and reward can be applied to create dopamine and do your daily activities and to achieve goals happily.

Example 1: Attending a Meeting at Work

- **Intention:** I am grateful to be with others and achieving collective goals for my company. I visualize gaining the outcome of the meeting happily.
- **Action:** Make every experience a happy experience. Start the meeting with a casual conversation to gain a bond with oxytocin. Do not let Thought Bugs impact you. Always use Power-Ups such a integrity, patience, and gratitude.
- **Reward:** Achieve the outcome of the meeting happily.

Example 2: Going to the Gym

- **Intention:** I love my body. It is my vehicle for this life, and I take care of it. I visualize a healthy body.
- **Action:** Make every experience a happy experience. I make it enjoyable by listening to music and talking to people in the gym.
- **Reward:** Achieve the fitness goals of a lean, healthy, 135 lb. body.

Example 3: Life Goal (e.g., writing a book)

- **Intention:** I can make a positive impact by sharing my knowledge to inspire and empower others to achieve greater happiness. Visualize the book launch.
- **Action:** Make every experience a happy experience. Writing a book is an enjoyable experience. It is like meditation. I love writing.
- **Reward:** Becoming a best-selling author and selling a million copies.

Example 4: Doing Housework

- **Intention**: This is a service to my family. Visualize aa clean house and a happy family.
- **Action**: Make every experience a happy experience. I ensure everything I do comes from a place of love. I listen to music while doing it to make it fun.
- **Reward**: Happy family!

Example 5: Talking to Someone

- **Intention**: I am grateful to be with you. How can I help?
- **Action**: Make every experience a happy experience. Listen consciously, ask questions, and uplift others.
- **Reward**: Build a real connection.

CHANGE YOUR TO-DO LIST TO YOUR "HAPPINESS EXPERIENCE LIST"

To-do lists may not be designed to trigger Happy Hormones. Instead, these lists have the potential to stress you out. The Happiness Experience List is an upgrade to the to-do list because it has two elements: the experience of doing something and a reward by accomplishment. To-do lists are designed only for the outcome of the effort. Until you finish a specific task, you could feel stress from it. I highly recommend setting a daily Happiness Schedule and doing them as happy experiences.

GETTING OVER ADDICTIONS

Dopamine is most notably involved in helping us feel pleasure as part of the brain's reward system. Sex, shopping, smelling cookies baking in the oven — all these things can trigger dopamine release, or a "dopamine rush." This feel-good neurotransmitter is also involved in reinforcement. That's why, once we try one of those cookies, we might come back for another one (or two, or three). The darker side of Dopamine is the intense feeling of reward people feel when they take drugs, such as heroin or cocaine, which can lead to addiction.[1]

The primary reason for addiction is pleasure-based dopamine. It could be an addiction to food, shopping, casual sex, pornography, alcohol, drugs, being a workaholic, gaming, etc. In these scenarios, the person is attached to dopamine pleasure and lacks healthy serotonin and endorphins. This is based on my experience. I had a strong desire for pornography, casual sex, and work at different times of my life. I overcame them successfully and got higher joy using balanced and healthy levels of serotonin, endorphins, dopamine, and oxytocin.

I see serotonin and endorphins as clean hormones for your health. Dopamine pleasures are temporary and overdoing it can cause health and life problems. Before Happiness Mountain, I used to entertain very high dopamine-based pleasures, and I was not happy inside. With the understanding of Happy Hormones, I created a fulfilling life without compromising my joy by using serotonin and endorphins together with dopamine and oxytocin in healthy ways.

Until you balance your life with all four Happy Hormones, dopamine pleasures can drive your life. An imbalanced life leads to a lack of fulfillment with your health, family, romance, finances, and much more. Do not compromise your valuable life for temporary joy. Always power up moderation. Enjoy true sustainable joy. Do not settle for an ordinary life. Live an extraordinary life using all four Happy Hormones.

LACK OF DESIRES

Some people do not have enough dopamine and hence no drive and motivation triggered by desires. It could be the desire for work, romance, sex, love, a fulfilled life, etc.

I will take an example to explain a common situation. When people get married, they desire love, intimacy, and sex. After a few years, it all goes away. In this situation, your dopamine and oxytocin levels fade away from the relationship. The worst case is when one partner still has desires and the other lacks them. A partner with more desires could cheat and be addicted to other things, like alcohol, casual sex, and pornography. It is essential to understand what is happening hormonally. In this situation, it is important to consciously work on creating a Happy Hormone balance.

When dopamine runs out, you need to put the effort into recreating your old desires and living a happy life. You can consult medical advice and counseling. The partner with more desires needs to balance themselves with serotonin and endorphins, and the other partner has to increase their desire with dopamine and oxytocin.

The same principle goes for a lack of desire without a meaningful purpose in life. Again, without a purpose you could dry out your dopamine and lose the drive-in life. Climb to the top of the Happiness Mountain and I am sure you will find your purpose and greatness in life.

OVERCOME PROCRASTINATION

You can use dopamine as a tool to finish a task you're procrastinating on. Start with setting the intention and visualizing the task and its results. Everything starts from your thoughts, and the intention and visualization step is essential to trigger dopamine and make yourself feel like doing the task is a happy experience. If it is a more enormous task, break it into smaller steps. Then, focus one step at a time, happily.

TIPS

- When you want the motivation to do something, set an intention and goals, and visualize results.
- When you do actions, say to yourself that you want to make a happy experience.
- Celebrate and acknowledge all your victories, big or small.
- Enjoy activities—such as food, alcohol, sex, games etc. that give you pleasure—in moderation.

- Through your awareness, measure your dopamine by evaluating whether you have the motivation, drive, and pleasure of doing what you are doing.

I trust you now understand the importance of dopamine and how to truly make every experience a happy one.

CHAPTER 28

OXYTOCIN = BOND + TRUST + LOVE

Feel-good intention	Primary techniques
Bond, trust, love	**Bond**: Make real connections with people **Trust**: Be respectful and believe in others **Love**: Live with love package: blessings, empathy, compassion, acts of kindness, and forgiveness

Oxytocin floods you with feelings of joy when you experience trust, bonding, and love. It could be with your partner, children, family, friends, pets, or community. Write down the names of a few people in your life whom you love, have a special bond with, and trust. Here is my list as an example:

- My two kids

- My former partner, who is my best friend
- My mom
- My brothers and sister
- The Happiness Mountain team and community
- My friends
- My work colleagues
- My mentors

Oxytocin plays a vital part in bonding with people. It gives joy that we often seek out in a relationship. This chemical can also contribute to a retreat after feeling that our trust has been betrayed.

These are the key attributes of Oxytocin:

- Create bonds to increase oxytocin and feel joy in relationships.
- Trust is a key component of a bond. Power up integrity to build trust with people.
- Bonding and trust cultivate your love for another person.

As humans, we need to bond with, trust, and love with other human beings, otherwise we can get depressed.

HOW TO TRIGGER OXYTOCIN

Your mind and body crave oxytocin. Nature created us with the need for human interaction. Do you remember the times when you felt you needed a loving relationship? This is because your desire for oxytocin is high. Quality relationships are the key to balanced oxytocin levels. These are some of the types of relationships that can generate oxytocin:

- A loving partner
- Kids

- Parents
- Family
- Mentors
- Friends you trust and with whom you can be yourself
- Good work relationships
- Being in groups with similar interests
- Pets
- Bonding with anyone you meet

As you can see, there are many ways you can create bonds, trust, and love to feel the magic of oxytocin.

IF YOU ARE SINGLE

You could feel the need for a relationship. At times, not having a relationship feels unsatisfactory to your needs. Understand more than anything that your mind and body are looking for oxytocin. Until you find the right partner, make sure you build other quality relationships with your family, friends, and groups with similar interests. You will not feel so much of a need for a love relationship by doing so.

Some people fulfill their oxytocin needs by getting a dog. A dog is man's best friend, and a good way to feel the joy of oxytocin.

Another primary hormone to consider is serotonin, which increases self-love. Be happy first, and you will attract the right partner quickly. Craving a relationship gives off negative energy, and your life will become harder. Staying happy and being yourself is the key to everything. With awareness, you can be happy in any circumstance, in a relationship or single.

ROMANTIC RELATIONSHIPS

With romance, we seek love, belonging, and pleasure. Your dopamine and oxytocin levels rise at the beginning of a romantic relationship. Dopamine is your desire for pleasure, and oxytocin is your love and belonging hormone. If your relationship is primarily based on desire-based dopamine, feelings of love and belonging eventually fade and you become less satisfied and unhappy. Have common interests and goals to create lasting relationships.

HOW TO AVOID CONFLICTS WITH FRIENDS

One day, one of my friends reached out and expressed disappointment with his close friend group over a request he made that nobody was taking seriously. There are many types of friends, and you should have expectations around that context. Types of friends can include:

- Social friends: To socialize and have fun with
- Spiritual friends: To talk about spiritual things with
- Uplifting friends: They lift your spirits
- Workout friends: Health- and body-conscious friends
- Work friends: Maintain a professional relationship with
- Friends who relate to a common interest, passion, or hobby
- Friends who offer a shoulder when you are sad

Having friends is a blessing. Understand oxytocin and make real connections with friends for lasting happiness.

TOUCH

Touch increases our bond and releases oxytocin. I give hugs to my family members quite often, which bring oxytocin to my loved ones and myself. I have reduced the hugs after COVID, but I hug others at every safe opportunity I get. Massages, cuddling, and making love are great ways to increase your oxytocin.

EXPECTATION THOUGHT BUG

The primary enemy of your oxytocin is the Expectation Thought Bug. As soon as you generate bonds, trust, and love, your Expectation Bug has room to take over your mental state. Oxytocin is a desired hormone. When strongly attached to bonds, trust, and love, you can get hurt if you feel like you do not have the other person's bond, trust, and love equally.

I had a period where I fell deeply in love, and we always had great ups followed by bad downs. We used to make love like rabbits and fight like dogs. It is always healthy to have some space between yourself and others, even your loved ones. You can enjoy love, bonds, and trust consistently by avoiding strong expectations. If not, your relationship will be short-lived, and you will have to deal with unhappiness.

TIPS

Here are a few ways that you can increase oxytocin:

- Create real connections with people by getting to know them better.
- Surround yourself with those who have similar beliefs.
- If people in your life are creating stress, you need to find a new circle!
- Join groups with people who share interests like your own. These can be anything from hiking groups to photography to business networks. Feeling that you belong to a tribe stimulates oxytocin.
- Spend more time with family without multitasking.
- Become actively involved as part of your community.

I trust you now understand the importance of oxytocin and how to create a joyful life by making real connections.

CHAPTER 29

SEROTONIN = ELEVATED MOOD + SELF-ESTEEM

Feel-good intention	Primary techniques
Boost mood & self-esteem	**Mood**: Primary actions • Go outside and connect with nature • Exposure to sun • Working out • Give gratitude • Do activities mindfully **Self-esteem**: Be yourself. Be authentic. Build your confidence in yourself.

Serotonin boosts your mood, emotions, and self-esteem. Having a great mood during the day is a blessing. Every morning, I go out for a walk, swim, or jog to improve my mood with high serotonin levels. This results in my day being better with other people too. If I do not continue my morning routine to keep my serotonin levels high, the chances of losing my mood and confidence significantly increase. Giving gratitude in the morning is a great way to boost your serotonin and feel good about life.

Serotonin is an important hormone that directly relates to your inner happiness. When you remove negative thoughts, you can produce more of this feel-good hormone. Happiness Mountain techniques can help you develop more serotonin and manage your moods and emotions more effectively, which is essential to creating happy experiences throughout the day. You know the opposite of the good-mood hormone: Cortisol, the stress hormone.

HOW TO TRIGGER SEROTONIN

Remember these simple ways to keep yourself in a good mood:

GO OUTSIDE AND CONNECT WITH NATURE

The biggest asset you have is nature, which is free. Many people forget about this and worry about the small real estate they are craving as their home. My home is nature and earth. Most of it is free, and I have the biggest home, and I am sharing it with eight billion amazing people. Now, close your eyes and think about the park and going for a walk to relax, or about the beach or the mountain you want to hike. Think of it as your own home. Enjoy the feeling.

EXPOSURE TO SUN

Exposure to either the sun or to bright light is another way to naturally increase serotonin levels. I go outside the house and feel the sunshine most days to get the serotonin trigger from sunshine. If you are exposed to a longer time in the sunshine, you may want to protect yourself with sun cream.

WORKING OUT

Working out at a slow space gives you serotonin and boosts your mood.

BE GRATEFUL FOR WHAT YOU HAVE

Serotonin is triggered when you think about the good you have in the present moment. Do daily gratitude affirmations in the morning so that your serotonin levels go up and you can be happier during the day.

BE MINDFUL

Mindfulness helps you stay in peace and in the present moment. That is a wonderful way to create a great mood.

MEDITATE

Meditation helps to calm your mind and generate serotonin.

BE YOURSELF

You are unique and extraordinary. When you love yourself enough to be yourself, your mood becomes perfect and raises your self-esteem. Take pride in how far you have come and know that where you are right now is perfect. This will set you up to reach your dreams and goals. Surrendering absolute control will also aid you in being more open to whatever the future holds.

DO NOTHING

Take it easy, let go, and relax. Our default mind always wants to hook up to something and run after it. With consciousness, you can relax by letting go and taking it easy. You might think doing nothing is easy, but for most people it is not. Train your mind to take breaks—do nothing.

BE CONSCIOUS OF NEGATIVITY

We have many negative moments in life:

- Stress
- Conflicts
- Criticism
- Agitation
- Temptation
- Rejection
- Impatience

These negative situations trigger Negative Thought Bugs. When I feel these negativities creeping into me, I immediately go for a walk or swim and consciously raise my serotonin levels. My mood elevates, and I can see a clear path and handle the situation.

In life, these situations will occur when we deal with other people, but it's a matter of being aware of the common culprits and consciously bringing yourself back to calmness. This will ensure you do not suffer any more than you need to. The Happiness Mountain app has a Quick Healing feature for you to calm your mind with. I recommend listening to the app while you are going for a walk or any other activity that connects you with nature. If you cannot go out of the house, take a shower and relax. Water is a part of nature that you can access inside your home.

Another critical point is that you should avoid big decisions while not in a good mood, feeling negative emotions. When your self-esteem is low, you may not make the best decisions. Your Self-Limiting Thought Bug could be in charge at this moment.

CORTISOL: STRESS HORMONE

When you are stressed, you are in a bad mood. Instead of Happy Hormones, you are now dealing with a stress hormone. The first thing you have to do is become conscious that you are undergoing stress, and cortisol may be triggered. Counter it and create a good mood by doing serotonin-triggering activities. Connect with nature to trigger serotonin so that the effects of the cortisol go away. You can even do a simple thing like taking a shower mindfully and connecting with the water. Adding a walk after would raise your mood further. Once your mood gets better, reflect on why you got stressed and see what you can do to overcome it. Find the root cause Thought Bugs that are creating the negative emotions and address them. Always be patient, and with good sleep you get more peace to handle any challenging matter.

TIPS

Here are a few more ways that you boost your mood:

- Choose positive thoughts. If your thoughts are negative, change how you think verbally (e.g., "I can't" becomes "I can").
- Expose yourself to sunlight, which will have the effect of producing serotonin naturally. It will help you look on the brighter side of things!
- Meditate.
- Practice yoga.
- Read a book, or listen to an audiobook, peacefully.
- Go for a nature walk.
- Learn to be alone in silence and to be happy with tranquility.
- Listen to relaxing music.
- Engage in prayers if this aligns with your spirituality.

- Engage in at least one activity daily to connect with nature.
- Exercise at a low intensity.
- Be authentic. Be yourself.

I trust you now understand the importance of serotonin and how to raise your mood and self-confidence.

CHAPTER 30
ENDORPHINS = HEALING + WELL-BEING

Feel-good intention	Primary techniques
Healing & Wellbeing	<ul><li>Runner's high</li><li>Vigorous-intense aerobic physical activity</li><li>Moderate-intense aerobic physical activity</li><li>Sing or dance</li><li>Laugh</li><li>Sauna</li><li>Sex</li></ul>

Endorphins are the body's natural pain relievers to help you with your healing and well-being. If you are feeling stressed, one thing you could do to relieve yourself is trigger endorphins.

Endorphins have the power to take your mind away from your

busy everyday life. It is a lifesaver and will help you avoid stress build-up. It will ensure a healthy heart and a happy life.

HOW TO TRIGGER ENDORPHINS

There are many activities that can help you to trigger endorphins.

AEROBIC PHYSICAL ACTIVITY

Endorphins as a Happy Hormones are overlooked. It happened to me as well. I was focusing on dopamine, serotonin, and oxytocin, and thought endorphins were something to trigger occasionally. I did not have enough moderate to intense activities to generate enough endorphins. Then I started aerobic exercises. When you do **aerobic physical activity, your body's oxygen demand increases, and your heart rate rises temporarily.** Aerobic activities with increased heart rate help to trigger endorphin release. For example, I started running on the treadmill and felt the runner's high. Another simple thing I do is go for a fast walk. Cycling in the summer is another great way.

After doing aerobics activities, I felt great. I felt like my mind and body were cleansed. My goal is to do one aerobic activity a day. I spend at least 20–60 minutes daily in aerobic activity for my happiness. Activities generating endorphins improved my health significantly; my skin looks younger and I feel lighter. This discovery taught me that all four Happy Hormones are equally important. The universe builds us with these hormones for a reason. If you want to feel true joy in life, make sure you trigger all four Happy Hormones (DOSE) daily. DOSE is the secret to living a happy and healthy life. As a bonus, you will also age gracefully.

Some important points to remember:

- Before doing aerobic activity, consult your doctor to see what fits for you.

- Using a wearable heart-rate monitoring device, you can get to know the different zones of your heart rate. That is an excellent way to track your moderate-intensity and vigorous-intensity physical activities. Most devices show:

1. Resting heart rate zone
2. Fat-burn zone, which is the moderate-intensity heart rate
3. Cardio zone, which is the vigorous-intensity heart rate
4. Peak zone, which is your peak heart-rate zone, in which you should not stay too long

- Before getting the wearable device, I used sweating to track moderate-intensity and vigorous-intensity aerobic physical activities.
- Spend at least 20–60 minutes daily for aerobic activity. It could be a quick 20-minute fast walk around the block or on the treadmill. Plan for 60 minutes or more of extensive aerobic activities thrice or more weekly. For example, join an aerobic exercise class and engage in a sport several times a week.
- A balanced life requires endorphins and doing at least one physical aerobic activity to complete the DOSE. Make these activities happy experiences. Feel the joy you get from endorphins after aerobic activity.

SAUNA

I go to the sauna at least four times during the week. A sauna gives a lot of health benefits and helps to release many Happy Hormones. When you sweat, you heal your mind and body. Spending time in the sauna improves cardiovascular functions. Sitting in the sauna is also a meditative activity that calms your mind. If you cannot run or do intense exercise, time in the sauna is an excellent way to cleanse your mind and body.

SING AND DANCE

Singing or dancing are things you can do daily. Focus on doing these simple activities that we are gifted with. I dance daily at home. I play music and dance while cooking or folding clothes, or anytime I feel like it. Don't wait for special occasions to dance or sing. Do it as an endorphin-generating happiness activity. Try to dance for five minutes or more daily. These simple things make your life beautiful, healthy, and happy.

LAUGH

Laughing is another gift that can generate endorphins. Watch more comedies and laugh. Read jokes and laugh. Laugh with your family and friends. Spend more time with friends who make you giggle.

SEX

Sex is another gift. Having good sex gives you endorphins. Having sex will provide you with more oxytocin and enhance your bonding. If you do not have enough sex after marriage, you can discuss it with your partner and increase your frequency of having sex to generate endorphins and live a happy and healthy life.

SEROTONIN AND ENDORPHINS

Serotonin improves your well-being by enhancing your mood. Endorphins help you with well-being through pain and stress relief. If you live a busy life, much stress is built up, knowingly or unknowingly. Healing by doing endorphin-generating activities is necessary for your well-being. Most activities generate more than one Happy Hormone. For example, exercising can generate serotonin, improve mood, generate endorphins, and heal your mind and body. Go on a hike and feel both endorphins and serotonin. Hike with friends and get oxytocin. Set a goal during a hike and have dopamine.

TAKE ADVANTAGE OF THE JOY THAT ENDORPHINS BRING TO YOUR LIFE.

When did you last do a physical activity until your heart rate increased and you sweated? I like to keep my body comfortable, and I was not doing that. I did not know what I was missing: endorphins. Then I discovered the healthy and happy endorphin high. Now I cannot stop doing it because it feels so good, and my health is at its best. Why do we tend not to do moderate to intense exercise? A valid reason could be medical conditions. Then it would be best if you talked to your doctor. If you do not have a medical condition preventing moderate to intense exercise, perhaps you aren't used to it. I overcame it by joining aerobic exercise classes so that I was motivated by everyone else in the room. Once you get the joy of runner's high, you start loving it. Get out of your comfort zone and make it happen. Believe it or not, once you do it right you get lots of joy out of it. Endorphins are non-desire-based Happy Hormones with only positive impacts. After an endorphin high, take a nice shower—you will feel amazing in your mind and body.

DESIRE BASED AND NON-DESIRE BASED HORMONES

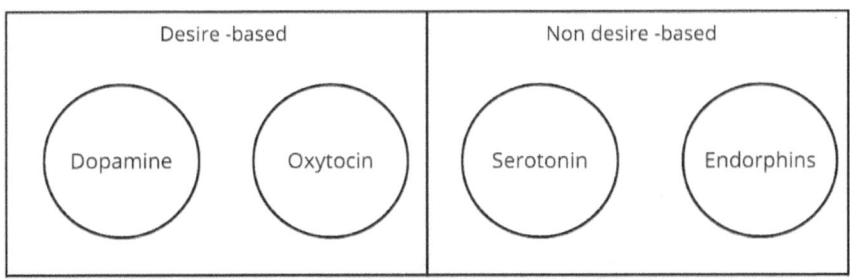

Balanced Life

Your healing and well-being are enhanced by non-desire-based serotonin and endorphins. People love dopamine and oxytocin because they are desire-based. Since serotonin and endorphins are non-desire based, people tend to avoid doing them and have health and stress problems in life. Going for a walk outdoors is simple and gives a lot of serotonins. Dancing, sex, laughing, and physical activity are great gifts to generate endorphins. Training the body to enjoy more non-desire-based serotonin and endorphins will make you balanced and truly happy, inside and out. Focus on all four Happy Hormones to live the best life! Get your daily DOSE of happy hormones.

CHAPTER 31
FEEDING HAPPY HORMONES IN UNHEALTHY WAYS

You can get joy from Happy Hormones with activities such as alcohol, pornography, drugs, casual sex, and video games. The purpose of this chapter is not to judge, but to encourage awareness. Awareness will help you design a moderate, healthy, and happy life.

ALCOHOL

Alcohol has a powerful effect on dopamine activity in the brain. When we drink, the brain's so-called reward circuits are flooded with dopamine.

This produces euphoric feelings—or what we recognize as feeling "buzzed."

drugrehab.com (13 Aug 2022)

Alcohol triggers dopamine, which feels good. The more alcohol you consume, the more it becomes one of your primary means of experiencing happiness. But alcohol is highly addictive. If you are a social drinker, have awareness and practice moderation.

PORNOGRAPHY

Sex, masturbation, and viewing pornography will ALL cause our brains to produce dopamine and ultimately crave more of it. We can become addicted to pornography for precisely that reason. Regular use of pornography will eventually lead to a craving for the dopamine that comes from using it.

everaccountable.com (22 Aug 2022)

Watching porn generates dopamine. Watching too much can get a person addicted to fulfilling sexual desires through it. Porn creates excitement by watching different people and different sexual activities. Your mind remembers this data. This could lead to problems with a partner or spouse, and enjoying sex in the real world. Porn can lead to relationship issues. Your ability to enjoy committed, intimate relationships can be compromised by an addiction to pornography.

DRUGS

Drugs can trigger the production of dopamine and serotonin. They can alter your mood, lead to pleasurable activities such as sex and make you feel happy—until their effect wears off.

Some drugs make your dopamine levels so high that real-world things will not give a similar level of joy, and your mind will keep asking for the higher levels you can only satisfy with drugs. That is how people get addicted to them.

. . .

The darker side of dopamine is the intense feeling of reward people feel when they take drugs, such as heroin or cocaine, which can lead to addiction.

health.harvard.edu (22 Aug 2022)

Your focus will shift away from what matters in life, such as your health, family, life goals etc. Also, problems are created by a lack of focus in life while taking drugs. You could end up with a lot of worries and unhappiness. Then more and more drugs are needed to close your mind to the real world, and they can waste your valuable life.

Suppose you have already taken drugs for recreational purposes and want to minimize or get out of them. In that case, one of the techniques you can do is to create a balanced life by adding joy to your life by doing serotonin and endorphins-triggering activities. You can learn more about serotonin and endorphins in the Happiness Experience Three section of the book.

CASUAL SEX

Sexual desire produces dopamine, the feel-good hormone and neurotransmitter for your mind's reward system. You are motivated to fulfill the desire, and when that desire is quenched, the dopamine subsides and you become calm.

Pleasure is registered in your memory, and thoughts are spawned from memories of having sexual activities with different partners. The mere thought of a specific pleasure can activate dopamine. This can lead you to connect with the same person or activity that previously rewarded you. Having multiple sexual partners can stem from this cycle of desire and reward. The lingering side effects of intimate, casual relationships can upset the balance of happiness and energy and include worry, anxiety, and other negative emotional and real-world consequences. The person's ability to be in a committed relationship can be challenged because they are addicted to dopamine generated from different casual sex experiences. Their mind looks for experiences with different people.

VIDEO GAMES

Video games are created with dopamine hits as a design principle to make players achieve goals. If you get addicted to this type of dopamine, you could miss the other parts of your beautiful life. Being aware of the dopamine pleasure and practicing balance and moderation will help you enjoy video games in a healthy manner.

PLEASURE VS LIFE GOALS

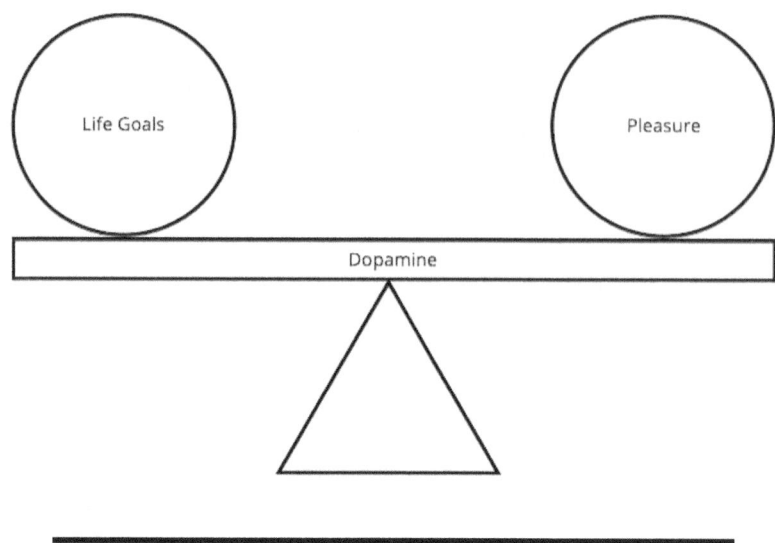

Dopamine Balance - Goals vs Pleasure

Dopamine is the Happy Hormone that brings joy from both pleasure and motivation. It's the motivation that allows you to achieve goals. When you use dopamine too much for pleasure, you lack the drive to achieve life goals. If you engage in too many pleasurable activities, like alcohol, sex, and drugs, you could get addicted to pleasure-based dopamine. Conversely, you may become a workaholic if you are too focused on achieving your goals. You have to be wise about how you get joy from dopamine.

A healthy balance between pleasure and goal achievement is the best approach. Be moderate with both. I use the following two principles:

- Seek a balance between pleasure-based dopamine and goal-based dopamine
- Get joy from all four types of Happy Hormones and do not get addicted to dopamine-based joy

HAPPINESS MOUNTAIN

Master your awareness about Happy Hormones and you can easily live a joyful life.

Happiness Experience Four: Living with Inner Happiness

CHAPTER 32
HOW TO GAIN INNER HAPPINESS

After many years of research, I found Inner Happiness. I will share what I discovered about it and how to gain it. Inner Happiness comes with a bonus. Once I became happy inside, everything in my outer world became happy. It is fascinating how humans are created. Everything changes when we are happy inside, and we can quickly become happy outside. Then I realized there is no such thing as only becoming happy from the outside. You become truly happy only when you are happy from the inside out. To truly become happy inside, you must understand the energy and your Higher Self you will learn about in this chapter. Then you can consciously adjust your vibration to stay in peace, harmony, and inner happiness. With inner happiness, you are grounded with stability and become resilient to outer-world matters.

YOU IN THE UNIVERSE

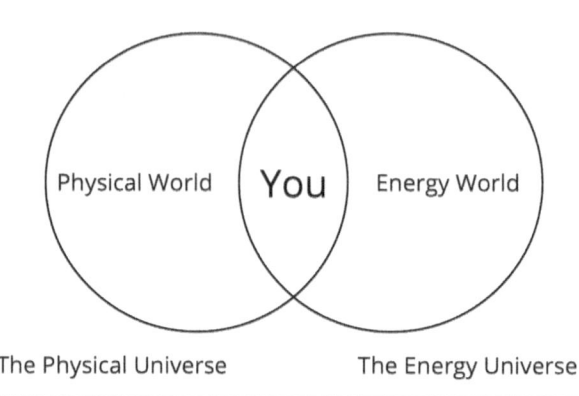

You have two worlds, the physical one and the energy one. Your life is part of both worlds. There could be many interpretations for the universe and you. I optimize Happiness Mountain's interpretation of the universe for happiness. There are many dimensions in the universe that are not part of the scope of Happiness Mountain, which intends to bring your awareness to the energetic and physical dimensions of the universe to consciously create a happy and fulfilled life.

PHYSICAL WORLD

The physical universe is vast, and we mostly know about earth. We have incomplete knowledge of many other planets and galaxies in the universe. You see and interact with only a fraction of the physical universe, which is your physical world.

Your physical world is your family, work, friends, communities, cities, countries you live in and visit, and physical assets, including cars, houses, money, etc. You can see the physical world with your five senses: sight, hearing, touch, smell, and taste. They act as your communication system to interact with and enjoy the physical world.

ENERGETIC WORLD

Three Levels of Energy

The energetic universe is enormous; you interact with and know a fraction of it, which is your energetic world. The energetic universe consists of three types of energies: foundational, advanced, and universal. Foundation-level energy is your positive and negative energy. The advanced energy level is life energy that you consume from the universe and emit to the universe. At a given time, your energy footprint represents your vibration. You have a core vibration and intermittent vibration. The mastery level is universal energy, the energy of the universe. Everyone and everything are connected in the energetic universe through universal energy.

Universal energy is free to take. The secret to getting it fresh is your vibration, beliefs, and consciousness, which you will learn details of in later chapters. To work with energy, you must understand who you are in this universe.

WHO ARE YOU?

The next step to gaining inner happiness is understanding *you*. Who are you? You are a creation of the universe with four distinct dimensions. Human design is complex. Let's simplify it so you can better manage yourself for greater happiness. Inner happiness operates at a mastery level. Therefore, I expect you to be ready for the deeper discussions and understanding that will make you strong.

YOU
Creation with four dimensions

1. Higher Self
Values, Beliefs, Purpose
(selfless)

2. Inner Self
Inner Talk, Thoughts, Seeking

3. Physical Self
Identity, Body, Actions

4. Lower Self
Desires, Anger, Judgments
(Selfish)

Definition of You

Your four dimensions are all interconnected. Please note that this is Happiness Mountain's definition of *you*.

HIGHER SELF

Your Higher Self is the most powerful dimension of you. Many people need to learn how to access their Higher Selves. Fortunately, you will learn how to access yours in the next chapter. Your Higher Self is selfless. You will not feel stress, worries, or fear—the low vibrations—once you establish your connection with your Higher Self. Your Higher Self is connected to the energetic universe.

INNER SELF

Self-talk is a crucial part of your Inner Self. It is your expression of the physical world to yourself. You see the physical world and interpret it with your Inner Self. Thoughts are significant parts of your Inner Self. The default behavior of your Inner Self is always seeking something to do. Your mind wants to jump from one thought to another. There are two forms of thoughts:

- Random Thought - Random thoughts drain your energy
- Intentional Thought Intentional thoughts power your energy up

PHYSICAL SELF

The Physical Self is your name, your body, how you dress, how you talk, and what you do. Others can see your Physical Self. Your Physical Self is a partial reflection of your Inner Self. It helps you to express your Inner Self in the physical world. You must maintain your Physical Self well, because if you do not, it will impact your Inner Self and Inner Happiness. Maintaining good health to make sure your Physical Self is supporting your overall well-being.

LOWER SELF

Your Lower Self is selfish. It is deeply connected to the Physical World. Some of the attributes of the Lower Self are:

- Anger
- Pride
- Desire
- Fear
- Grief
- Apathy
- Guilt
- Shame

The Lower Self brings you unhappiness. One who has not discovered their Higher Self does not know how to get out of their Lower Self and their suffering. The one who knows Inner Happiness does not allow the Lower Self to gain control of their life. Once you master your Higher Self, you can live a peaceful life harmoniously with everyone and everything in the universe.

WHAT IS INNER HAPPINESS?

Inner Happiness is the peace, harmony, clarity, and resiliency you gain by connecting with your Higher Self. When your Inner and Physical Selves align with your Higher Self, you gain Inner Happiness. When your inner and physical selves align with your Lower Self, you lose Inner Happiness.

To gain Inner Happiness, you must be aware of your four dimensions and how to operate them.

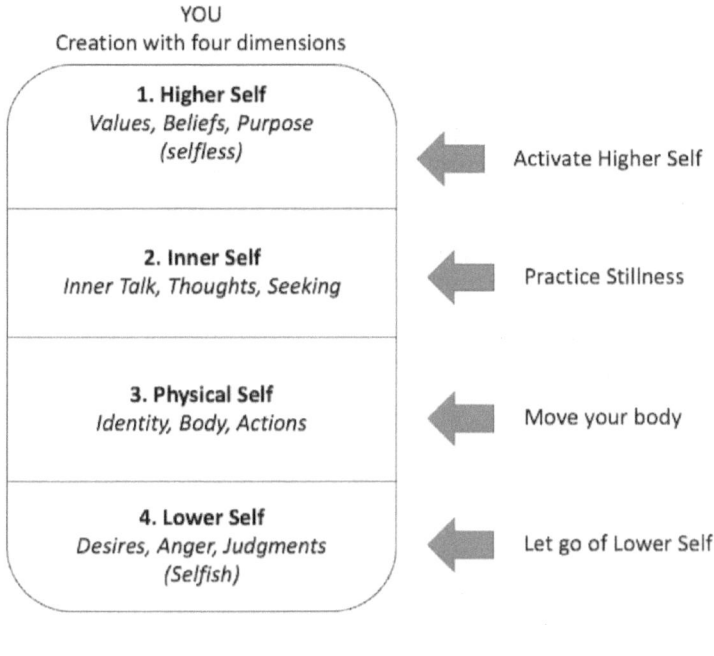

How to Manage Dimensions

Now let's look at how you should operate your four dimensions for Inner Happiness:

ACTIVATE HIGHER SELF

Activating your Higher Self is the foundation for Inner Happiness, discovering your greatness, and life fulfillment. The next chapter will give you details on how to activate your Higher Self.

PRACTICE STILLNESS

It is vital to bring stillness to your Inner Self. Do that through meditation, mindfulness, and serotonin-generating activities. Please refer to the mindfulness chapters in this regard.

MOVE YOUR BODY

Your mind and body work together, and having an active body is essential for Inner Happiness. Yoga is very good for the mind and body. Do some yoga daily. If you are not used to doing it alone, sign up for a class. Aerobic exercise is also essential for your well-being. Here are some good aerobic exercises:

- Swimming
- Cycling
- Using an elliptical trainer
- Walking
- Rowing
- Running
- Jumping rope

LET GO OF YOUR LOWER SELF

You learned how to let go of your Lower Self in the Negative Thought Bugs section. Now you can add more context to it and do more cleansing. Use this affirmation: "I always stay with my Higher Self, and I let go of my Lower Self." Start noticing your Lower Self when it comes up. As soon as you see that it is your Lower Self acting up, stop that thought chain and replace it with your purpose. Have you yet to find your purpose? Don't worry. In the next chapter, you will learn more about how to unlock your purpose and reprogram the Lower Self with your Higher Self.

CHAPTER 33
CONNECT TO YOUR HIGHER SELF

Living with a higher vibration is a blessing. You feel inner peace. You are resilient to what is happening around you, especially since the world is attracting a lot of negative energies. You must protect your inner peace with your higher vibration. You can only be at your higher vibration with your Higher Self. You can activate your Higher Self by establishing:

- Higher Self beliefs
- Higher Self values
- Higher Self purpose

Oftentimes people do not have clarity of their beliefs, values, and purposes for happiness, which causes their Lower Self to take control of their life. Let's change that for you. Let set up a great set of beliefs, values, and purposes for Inner Happiness. You can always add more or make some adjustments. Please note that these are not religious beliefs, and they are not intended to conflict with any religious, cultural, or political views. These beliefs, values, and purposes are purely defined for your happiness and well-being.

HIGHER SELF BELIEFS

The following are nine Inner Happiness beliefs will take you to your higher vibration. You have to believe in them and then practice them.

1. Take care of your mind and body first.
2. Objectively experience life's duality.
3. Accept impermanence.
4. Be in service to others.
5. Be yourself, be authentic.
6. Surround yourself with quality people.
7. Stop energy drops and create.
8. Maintain a higher consciousness with mindfulness.
9. Believe in yourself and your higher power.

This chapter will give you foundational knowledge. Then you need to apply your new knowledge to your day-to-day life. After practice, these become new patterns in your mind, and you can enjoy Inner Happiness for your whole life.

Joining weekly Happiness Mountain mentoring sessions will help keep the focus and gain Inner Happiness faster. You can find them on the Happiness Mountain website.

1. TAKE CARE OF YOUR MIND AND BODY FIRST

You need a healthy mind and active body to feel Inner Happiness. An uplifted mind and body are the key to connecting with your Higher Self. Even though we separate mind and body in language, they are interconnected and work as one.

You already learned in the Positivity chapter how to start the day using Happiness Mountain's recommended five-step recharge. For Inner Happiness, these are a must:

1. Stretch and wake up your body with some yoga moves.

2. Read your affirmations and bless the world.
3. Give gratitude to what you have and the people in your life.
4. Write your Happiness Schedule.
5. Do 5–10 minutes of meditation.

The next step is to balance your Happy Hormone DOSE by increasing your serotonin and endorphins. Serotonin is key to Inner Happiness. Endorphins heal your mind-body. You need an energized mind-body to do everything else.

Bonus: You can age happily.

2. OBJECTIVELY EXPERIENCE LIFE'S DUALITY

How do you experience life objectively as opposed to subjectively? Life is all about duality.

- Light and dark
- Profits and loss
- Life and death
- Fame and defamation
- Peace and war
- Economic prosperity and recession
- Comfort and discomfort

Say the economy is going into recession. If you are upset and worried about its impact, you are experiencing it *subjectively*. If you already know the duality of the economy, you look at it *objectively* and act accordingly. Some people may say good things about you, and some may say bad things. Sometimes you make profits, and sometimes you make losses. Parts of the world have had wars before, and came to peace afterwards. In our families, we see births and deaths. Do not become the subject of the situation by being overly attached to good things or being overly resistant when things are bad. Step back and look at the duality objectively, and experience everything with patience. Always stay with your Higher Self and remain resilient to the duality.

3. ACCEPT IMPERMANENCE

Everything is impermanent, including your life, thoughts, and circumstances. Say you had a bad day. It is OK. You know it is not going to be permanent.

Are you going live forever? No. You will die, and you are not taking anything with you. Do you have living parents? Now think about your grandparents. Do you know their names? Think about your great-grandparents and great-great-grandparents. What were their names? Most of the time, we remember one or two generations above us. Now think about yourself. After two generations, people may not know you, and your existence will disappear.

Now think about World War II and COVID-19 lockdowns. They were also not permanent. Think about someone you loved who died. Now think about a time you or someone else lost their job and are doing well with a new one. Think about a worry you had before it is completely forgotten about. Think about a conflict you had with someone who is no longer significant to your life. Everything about our life is impermanent. Take it easy and enjoy the journey.

4. BE IN SERVICE TO OTHERS

Live as if your primary purpose is to serve others. Get used to the question, "How can I help?" Try to use this sentence at least once a day. When you are in service to others, you feel good. Your stress goes away. You naturally connect to your Higher Self. Make your mindset change to become service-oriented. Here are some of the changes I made:

- In the morning, I say an affirmation that I am in service to others.
- I accept all my responsibilities at home as a service to my family.
- I accept work responsibilities at my company as a service to customers, co-workers, and partners.
- I do community service to increase my service to others.

Service orientation includes a better understanding of others' needs and concerns. Listen to them. Do it with positive energy. Do not create negative energy in people's lives. Forgive other people's Thought Bugs by staying with your Higher Self. Power up and serve with integrity, patience, acceptance, and love. Make a positive impact in others' lives.

5. BE YOURSELF, BE AUTHENTIC

Put simply, authenticity means you're true to your personality, values, and spirit, regardless of the pressure that you're under to act otherwise. You're honest with yourself and with others, and you take responsibility for your mistakes. Your values, ideals, and actions align. As a result, you come across as genuine, and you're willing to accept the consequences of being true to what you consider to be right.[1]

It is important to be true to yourself to have Inner Happiness. When you are yourself, your mood goes up and you produce serotonin. Your mood is fundamental to your happiness. People tend to live the way others want them to when they're under social pressure. The cost of not being yourself with authenticity is high for your happiness and well-being.

Some people may not like parts of your authentic self, that's OK. The critical point is not to exercise your Anger Thought Bug towards people who dislike your authentic behavior. Be respectful of others' beliefs even when they are not respecting yours.

When you become yourself with authenticity, you have to be conscious of cultures, beliefs, religions, other people's feelings and laws in different countries.

The following is a good article from the *Harvard Business Review* referring to being yourself in the workplace.

But the honest sharing of thoughts, feelings, and experiences at work is a double-edged sword: Despite its potential benefits, self-disclosure can backfire if it's hastily conceived, poorly timed, or inconsistent with cultural or organizational norms—hurting your reputation, alienating employees, fostering distrust, and hindering teamwork.[2]

Being authentically yourself should be practiced as your Higher Self with Positive Power-Ups, which will impact others and allow you to live with Inner Happiness.

6. SURROUND YOURSELF WITH QUALITY PEOPLE

Nobody is perfect. At the same time, you have to choose to associate with those who do not take away your Inner Happiness. If you associate with people who have lots of negative energy, there is a higher chance of you being affected by their energy. For example, if you are with someone who gets angry or judges others all the time, you lose your Inner Happiness too. They are not bad people, but if you want Inner Happiness you must choose who you associate with carefully. Everybody has a vibe and energy. The people surrounding you influence you with their energies.

Whoever comes into your energy space will affect your Inner Happiness positively or negatively. It is essential to associate with friends and groups that support each other. Also, be a good person and support the people around you.

You must consciously look at whether you have enough mentors. Every successful person has mentors, including me. Check your list of mentors and do what is needed to ensure you have enough for the various areas of your life. A mentor should already be successful in the domain you get advice from. I mentor people for happiness and get mentoring for areas in which I am not an expert.

7. STOP ENERGY DROPS AND CREATE

To gain Inner Happiness with your Higher Self, you must learn to manage energy.

You have the power to create. At the same time, your mind tends to resist many things. It could happen during a disagreement with someone. It could get in the way of achieving a goal. Every time you work with resistance, there is an energy drop. Develop the skill to catch the energy drops created by resistance. Once you notice the opposition, immediately step back from it. Look for possibilities to create a better outcome and let go of the resistance.

Your energy is the most valuable currency you have. You can lose your energy from

- Your negative thoughts
- Your negative beliefs
- Your negative behaviors
- Your negative actions
- Resistance to others

Look at these five areas and clean up to amplify your Inner Happiness. Your Self-Limiting Bug could be the reason for some of the energy drops. Now it is time to let go of your Self-Limiting Bug and vibrate with higher energy.

Negative energy prevention is always better than a cure. If you can catch the energy drop as soon as it enters you, you can avoid the

Negative Thought Bugs altogether. Always remember to stop resisting and see the possibilities to create better outcomes.

Your new skill is to observe thoughts that cause energy drops. You can maintain high resiliency by believing you can see and let go of them. Consistently stay in a creative space and let go of any energy-dropping thoughts entering your mind.

8. MAINTAIN A HIGHER CONSCIOUSNESS WITH MINDFULNESS

Consciousness is the awareness of your internal state of mind and external factors and choosing how to respond positively. For example, when you get angry, you cannot be conscious because you lose your awareness and the choice to act positively. A busy mind loses consciousness and attracts negativity. When you lose consciousness, you lose Inner Happiness. To gain consciousness, you need to keep your mind clean with values, beliefs, and purpose. By climbing Happiness Mountain, you can gain a higher state of consciousness.

Maintain consciousness by being mindful while you do daily activities. As discussed in the Mindfulness Power-Up section, keep the brain waves in the Alpha range and slow down activities to increase mindfulness. Remember what the Navy SEALs say: "Slow is smooth, smooth is fast."

Positive Power-Ups help you to reach your higher consciousness. Your negative Thought Bugs bring down your energy and keep you suffering in the rat race. As long as you entertain your Thought Bugs, you are in suffering because you can not open your higher consciousness.

Higher Consciousness	
Mindfulness	
Love	
Integrity	
Gratitude	Power to create the life you love
Acceptance	
Patience	
Moderation	
Uplift	
Lower Energies ⬇	
Anger Bug	
Cravings Bug	
Expectation Bug	
Fear Bug	Suffering
Judgmental Bug	
Worry Bug	
Do-it-Later Bug	
Self-Limiting Bug	

Consciousness - *Power-Ups vs Thought Bugs*

Many people in the world's population are living at a lower energies. Staying in low frequencies results in suffering or just getting by. To live in Inner Happiness with peace, joy, love, and peace, you need to raise your vibration.

By activating Higher Self consciousness, you can live a happier life with power to create the life you love.

9. BELIEVE IN YOURSELF AND YOUR HIGHER POWER

You can use multiples of your life energy by believing in yourself. The amount of power generated depends on how strongly you believe. The more you believe, the more power you will obtain.

- Believe in yourself
- Believe in what you want to achieve
- Believe in the power of energy

We all have enough energy to last until we die. Some achieve greatness and live happy, healthy, and wealthy lives, while others do not. One of the factors is your ability to believe and draw energy for the energetic universe. There is an immense about of fresh energy in the universe. The way to get energy from the universe is by believing. In Happiness Experience Six: Life Fulfillment with happiness, health, and wealth, doing what you love, you will learn three energy laws:

- Law of vibration
- Law of attraction
- Law of creation

The pre-condition to work with the above energy laws is your belief in yourself and what you want to create, and the energy in the universe.

HIGHER SELF VALUES

You already learned the core values in Happiness Experience One: Living with full positive energy.
Energy Amplifiers
Gratitude
Uplift
Energy Stabilizers
Mindfulness
Integrity
Energy Protectors
Love
Acceptance
Patience

Moderation

Keep practicing and they will gradually become part of your core values, and your vibration will change.

HIGHER SELF PURPOSE

My purpose is to make the world a happier place by helping people to overcome negative energy and be happy and fulfilled in their lives.

You can follow a similar pattern and set your purpose to make the world a happier place, and define how you give back:

 "My purpose is to make the world a happier place by [your unique giveback]."

Once you define your beliefs, purposes, and values, and live according to them, you naturally gain Inner Happiness with your Higher Self.

Happiness Experience Five: Find Your Greatness

CHAPTER 34

HOW TO DISCOVER YOUR GREATNESS

Service to others leads to greatness.

You have greatness. The question is, how do you discover it? There is only one way: serving others by giving back. The main question is how to do it. We all know that donations and volunteering are good ways of giving back. Is that enough to discover your greatness? Doing good deeds and finding your greatness have similarities, but there is a significant difference. Before Happiness Mountain, I gave back when I could. I considered this to be a good deed. How I gave back did not result in any notable shift in my life, such as discovering my greatness. By climbing Happiness Mountain, I understood the true meaning of giving back to discover greatness. I changed my life to live with gratitude and serve others. That changed everything.

To give back and discover your greatness, you must act with a higher consciousness. Giving back is a good deed that will not take you to a high enough vibration to experience the greatness in you.

> You can choose a life of comfort or a life of service and adventure; which one, when you are ninety, will you be most proud of?
>
> —JEFF BEZOS, FOUNDER OF AMAZON

Giving back as a good deed is an activity. Being in service to others is a mindset change, together with transforming every action that aligns to it. By doing so, your vibration changes and starts attracting great things to your life. I trust you want to live at your best in this life and to discover your greatness. Happiness Mountain's methodology defines how to do that. Discovering your greatness involves three aspects:

- Activate your Higher Self
- Do the nine givebacks
- Accept rewards to do more good

Now let's understand each aspect so that you can discover your greatness.

ACTIVATE YOUR HIGHER SELF

Greatness is when you give back wholeheartedly with your Higher Self. If you give back with returns as the primary motive, you may get the Cravings Thought Bug and stress, worry, and unhappiness. Even if you give back successfully, you will lose your Inner Happiness. For example, you should not seek praise when donating. Even if you get a negative response after you give, you should be able to bless and forgive everyone involved. When you give, always stay in your Higher Self. You are here to serve as many people as you can.

Focus on staying in your greatness when you serve through your business. More good people should serve by creating businesses and making the world a better place. Some good people think making money by giving back is wrong. Money is a resource to do more good. If you have negative thoughts about money, use one of the affirmations I learned from author and motivational speaker Jack Canfield:

- The more money I have, the more good I can do in the world.
- The more I do what I love, the more money flows into my life.
- Whenever I give away money, it comes back to me multiplied.
- Money is the root of all good things.
- I live in an abundance universe and money always come to me easily and effortlessly.

DO THE NINE GIVEBACKS

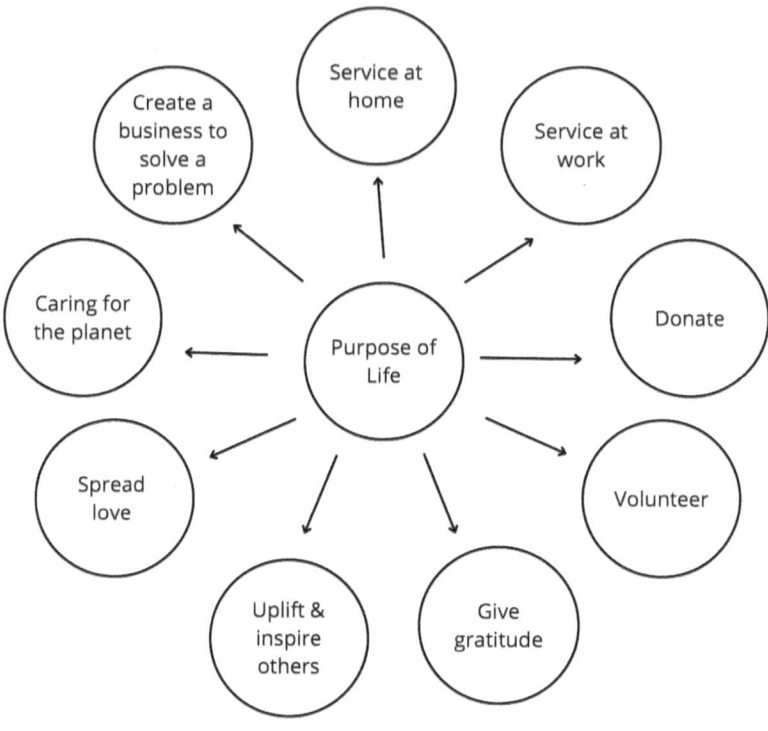

Nine Givebacks

Do as many of the nine givebacks as possible. The more types you give, the more your greatness starts showing up. Each giveback opens a different perspective of your mind:

1. Service at home
2. Service at work
3. Donate
4. Volunteer

5. Give gratitude
6. Uplift and inspire others
7. Spread love
8. Care for the planet
9. Create a business, solve a problem

Lots of people have asked me how to find the purpose of life. The answer is to choose from the nine types of givebacks. When you are giving back and living connected to your Higher Self, you will discover your purpose of life.

ACCEPT REWARDS TO DO MORE GOOD

When you give more, you receive more than you can imagine. Those are your rewards for your givebacks. You become entitled to great:

- Happiness
- Health
- Wealth
- Respect
- Self-esteem
- Life fulfillment
- Abundance

With all the above, you will find your greatness. Accept those rewards in a humble way and increase your ability to help more people. You will truly feel whole and complete.

CHAPTER 35
YOUR NINE GIVEBACKS

Let's do an evaluation where you are giving back. Filling in the below check boxes brings your awareness to each area. Think about each area and tick the corresponding box.

	Doing	To Do
Service at home	☐	☐
Service at work	☐	☐
Donate	☐	☐
Volunteer	☐	☐
Give gratitude	☐	☐
Uplift & inspire others	☐	☐
Spread love	☐	☐
Caring for the planet	☐	☐
Business to solve a problem	☐	☐

When you give back, it is important to have the right mindset. Let's look at each one of them to set a Higher Self mindset of giving.

SERVICE AT HOME

You give back consciously or unconsciously every day. For example, you do many things for your family to improve their lives. If you make breakfast for your family, it is a giveback. Give back with love and care as your service to your family. Change your mindset from "performing responsibilities or housework" to "serving your family with your greatness." What is the difference? Your energy. Giving back as a service gives off a higher vibrational energy than "doing housework or responsibilities," which could lead to stressful energy. When you perform a task as a service, your family will feel your great love and your presence will become pleasurable. Their minds will be healed and you will not add more stress to their lives. You will feel your greatness. It starts at your home.

SERVICE AT WORK

Every business provides a service to its customers. When you go to work, you are part of the service it provides, but you may not feel this if you are not directly involved with customers. If you look at the whole process of your business, you can see how you help the company. You can go to your workplace for your paycheck, or you can be in service to your workplace at a higher vibration. To discover your greatness, choose to be in service to your company. Your paycheck is gratitude from your company for your greatness.

DONATIONS

Consciously plan to make donations to the people who need your help. For example, you can donate to the food bank or directly to a person who needs food. Find a cause and donate.

VOLUNTEERING

You can find places to volunteer in your community. You have greatness. Act by going beyond your comfort zone and volunteer.

GIVING GRATITUDE

When you receive services and products from others, always offer gratitude. Whether you are paying money for the service or product does not matter—still, the people involved in providing them work hard to make it happen. Say a delivery person brings food to your door. They have to go to the restaurant on your behalf, wait there, and deliver the food to you. They spend their time for you. Time is the most valuable thing in this world. Looking at what you eat and thinking about how many people are involved in getting that food on your table is impressive. Think for a moment about the people involved and serve them back with your gratitude. Bless them to be successful in what they are doing. Discover your greatness by living at your higher vibration.

UPLIFT AND INSPIRE OTHERS

Words have energy. What you say matters to others. Always lift others up, as you learned in the Positivity Power-Up. Here are some reminders of how words can be powerful:

- "I think very highly of you."
- "I know you can do it, and I have faith that you'll be successful."
- "I am very happy and proud of you."
- "Stay focused, and you will be successful."
- "You are truly special."

Offer your uplifting words to others with your greatness. Give back uplifting words to everyone in your life: your partner, children, friends, work colleagues, and anyone you meet during the day.

SPREAD LOVE

Give love with your greatness. Please refer back to the Love chapter if you want to refresh your mind.

Love package = blessings, empathy, compassion, acts of kindness, and forgiveness.

One who practices and lives with love has the highest form of greatness. Do not emit dark energies to the universe; instead, be a light in the world.

CARE FOR THE PLANET

The planet takes care of you. The planet is your home. It is your responsibility to take care of the planet.

- **Reduce, reuse, and recycle:** Cut down on what you throw away. Follow the three Rs to conserve natural resources and landfill space.
- **Volunteer:** Volunteer for cleanups in your community. You can get involved in protecting your watershed, too.
- **Educate:** When you further your own education, you can help others understand the importance and value of our natural resources.
- **Conserve water:** The less water you use, the less runoff and wastewater that eventually end up in the ocean.
- **Choose sustainable:** Learn how to make smart seafood choices at www.fishwatch.gov.
- **Shop wisely:** Buy less plastic and bring a reusable shopping bag.
- **Use long-lasting lightbulbs:** Energy-efficient lightbulbs reduce greenhouse-gas emissions. Also flip the light switch off when you leave the room!
- **Plant a tree:** Trees provide food and oxygen. They help save energy, clean the air, and help combat climate change.
- **Don't send chemicals into our waterways:** Choose non-toxic chemicals in the home and office.
- **Bike more:** Drive less.

CREATE A BUSINESS TO SOLVE A PROBLEM

You are unique. You have excellent skills, passions, and life experiences that can help others greatly. How do you make an impact on others? You have two choices. You can share your experience as an individual and make an impact in the world, or you can create a business and help others.

By creating a business, you can serve more people. Your rewards are also higher with a business. Starting a business requires effort, but you learn many things on that journey. Creating a business means you develop yourself to another level. One of my intentions is to help people build businesses to positively impact the world.

There are light and dark energies. If the light energy does not create businesses, the dark will fill the gap and the world will become darker. Money has energy. Combine your light with money and positively impact the world. I encourage everyone to do more by being a part of a business. You do not have to start from scratch. You can help other founders by joining those companies and becoming a partial owner. Give your skillset to grow businesses that make the world a happier place. Connect with a company's purpose with your highest integrity, energy, and skills. Energize the company with what you are good at and discover your greatness.

PURPOSE OF LIFE

You are here on earth to serve. By connecting with your Higher Self and doing the nine givebacks, you will start feeling the greatness in you. You will discover your purpose and meaning of your life. Do it with integrity and mindfulness. The happiness you gain by giving back cannot be explained in words. It is something you can only discover by doing. You have your greatness in you. Enjoy life being the best version of yourself!

Happiness Experience Six: Life Fulfillment

CHAPTER 36
HOW TO ATTAIN FULFILLMENT

I heard the word *fulfillment* and all the good things about it throughout my life. I was missing a fundamental understanding of fulfillment, though. What is fulfillment, and how do you attain it? Since I did not know these fundamentals about fulfillment, I did not experience it before climbing Happiness Mountain. I acquired material things, but I still needed to be fulfilled. After climbing Happiness Mountain, I attained life fulfillment. I incorporated why, what, and how to achieve life fulfillment into the Happiness Mountain methodology so that anyone who doesn't understand it can get to know what it is and attain life fulfillment.

WHY FOCUS ON LIFE FULFILLMENT?

Let's talk about why you should focus on fulfillment:

- If you are not fulfilled, you might miss life's meaning and feel trapped in the rat race.
- You will suffer more within your mind even though you manage to get through life.

- You might do things to close your mind, such as becoming a workaholic, checking social media more, drinking, and staying in the rat race.
- You may feel that life is monotonous with dull, repetitive, and tedious feelings.
- You may not find your best version of yourself.

Eventually you become numb to that feeling and accept it as life. In the back of your mind, you may feel that you are not fulfilled. Let's see how you can close that gap and focus on your fulfillment and have Happiness Experience Six: Life Fulfillment with happiness, health, and wealth, doing what you love.

WHAT IS LIFE FULFILLMENT?

After carefully looking at life through my research, I realized that we become fulfilled if we satisfy the eight domains of our life. Those domains are called the Life Fulfillment Map. Two additional domains, romance and business, are optional; you may or may not want to fulfill them.

Domains	Intentions
Mind	Happy and peaceful mind
Body	Healthy active body
Personal interests	Do what you love
Family	Loving and caring family
Work	Serve others while enjoying work-life happiness
Social	A good relationship with friends, mentors, and community
Wealth	A satisfactory amount of wealth
Giveback	Make positive impacts by giving back
Optional	
Romance	Love and intimacy with your partner
Business	Business to serve the world and create more wealth

Life Fulfillment Map

You are intelligent. If you know what to focus on and what matters, you can fulfill those areas.

PRIORITIZE

You do not have to do it all at once. Prioritize what you want. Start with your mind and body domains, since those are fundamental to your happiness. Practicing Happiness Mountain methodology is your best choice for uplifting and fulfilling your mind and body. When you work on your mind, you will naturally work on your body, since the mind-body connection goes together.

To reprogram the mind for fulfillment, I give one domain three to six months. Along the way, you might lose fulfillment in some areas you already gained it in. That is OK. You know how to get back on track, since you have done it before. At the end, what matters is the balance in all domains.

FULFILLMENT VS PERFECTION

Your target should not be perfection. Life is not about being perfect. You may accept some areas as is and become fulfilled in a short period. Your mind always looks for what you don't have and becomes unfulfilled. You must train your mind to become fulfilled with what you have, and then work on improvements on top of your baseline. **Learn how to be happy with what you have while pursuing all you want.**

Make sure you do everything while living a balanced and joyful life. Improving your domains has to be a happy experience. If not, you need to use the correct principles of Happiness Mountain.

A SIMPLE PROCESS TO FULFILL DOMAINS

You learned how to get motivated to achieve results with dopamine. You can follow the three steps we discussed in the dopamine chapter:

1. **Intention:** Enjoy setting your intention and visualize your ideal results. You just created dopamine, motivation, and drive.
2. **Action:** Have fun listing your action steps. Make each action step a happy experience by taking each one with a positive attitude, resulting in further dopamine, motivation, and drive to continue.
3. **Reward:** When you've achieved your desired results, you will feel happier. Your dopamine levels will skyrocket. Celebrate for even more!

PHENOMENAL HAPPINESS

You can live a phenomenally happy life when you are fulfilled internally and externally.

Internal Happiness

Being internally happy means you are feeling:

- Positive about yourself and the world
- That stress and worries don't make you suffer
- The joy in life
- Inner happiness and peace
- Your greatness

When you are internally happy, you will feel **whole and complete**. So far, in practicing Happiness Mountain you have focused on becoming internally happy. It is like working out: you need to continue to maintain a state of internal happiness. Practicing Happiness Mountain's first five experiences will keep you internally happy. The good energy you get being happy will spread to your external world, and those you come into contact with will become happy too.

EXTERNAL HAPPINESS

Being externally happy means you're successful in the physical world:

- Money
- Career
- Relationships
- Home
- Material things such as cars, phones, clothes, etc.

We live in a materialistic world. To live a happy life, knowing how to create the life you desire in the physical world is important. Life is all about balance. You could decide to stay internally happy and give less significance to external success. That is OK. **Happiness Mountain recommends balance and being both internally and externally to become happy.**

"Physical world success" is a subjective term. Generally, if you can live a happy, healthy, and wealthy life in the physical world, you are living a successful life. Since we drive everything by fulfillment, you can define your physical-world success based on your fulfillment criteria. Always remember you have a unique path in this world. **Embrace your journey and wish others success in their journeys.**

HOW TO GAIN INTERNAL AND EXTERNAL HAPPINESS

INTERNAL

Your internal fulfillment is achieved by increasing wholeness by letting go of your Lower Self (e.g., anger, obsessions, judgments, etc.) and connecting with your Higher Self (e.g., love, gratitude, mindfulness, etc.)

Your Inner Self becomes complete when you accomplish your purpose by giving back and discovering your greatness.

Primary domains for internal happiness

- Mind
- Body
- Personal interests
- Giveback

These domains are under your control.

External

Your external fulfillment is related to success in the physical world. Primary domain for external happiness

- Wealth
- Work
- Family
- Social

These domains are not under your complete control.

There is a gray line between internal and external happiness since they influence each other.

Notes

- Rich vs Wealthy: You are rich if you have a lot of money. It could mean having money in banks and other assets like properties. But you may not have internal happiness with balance and mindset, with the freedom to enjoy money. If you are wealthy, you have both time and money freedom as well as internal happiness.
- Climbing Happiness Mountain will make you fulfilled both internally and externally.

PROGRESSING TOWARDS PHENOMENAL HAPPINESS

To become phenomenally happy, you need to clear internal and external fulfillment gaps. Focus on the internal first to quickly close the gap.

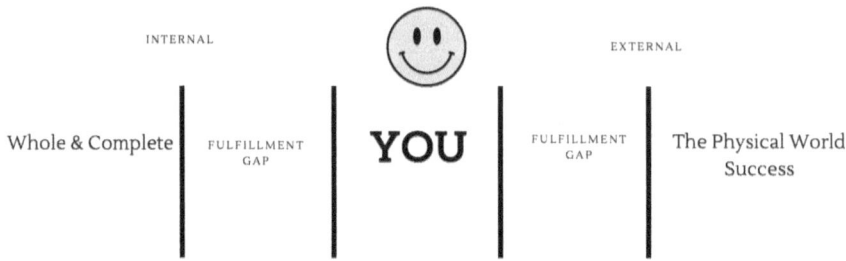

If you start from the external, you might look for perfection and what society or other people want you to do. Avoid that risk by starting to feel whole and complete internally. **When you become happy inside, you naturally become happy outside.** You will attract good things in the outer world when you are happy inside. Happiness Mountain is designed in such a way that you become happy inside first and then focus on external happiness. **Only if you are internally happy can you genuinely enjoy external success.** Let me give some examples:

- You may have a great job, but if you are not internally happy, you are not fulfilled and happy.
- You may have a good partner, but if you are not internally happy, you cannot see the goodness and the blessings of living with them.
- You may have great kids, but if you are not internally happy, you cannot see their uniqueness and may try to force your desires on them.
- You have a wonderful human life—if you are not internally happy, you do not see the value of it.

HAPPINESS MOUNTAIN

When you truly practice Happiness Mountain, you become happy internally, and you naturally become successful in the external world with what you got with less effort. I have seen this in my life, and in the lives of everyone who practices Happiness Mountain. The biggest mistake I have seen people make is focusing externally and never reaching internal fulfillment. Without internal fulfillment, they cannot enjoy external success. That is how people get lost in life and can't see its meaning. Practice **Happiness Mountain daily and focus internally first, and external success will come to you as your reward.**

PHENOMENAL HAPPINESS REALIZATION

When you are phenomenally happy, your internal and external worlds are in harmony, without conflicts. Once you complete the fulfillment gaps inside and outside, you will reach the top of Happiness Mountain.

We are all on different journeys. Yours differs from your parents', your siblings', and your friends'. When I divorced, I thought my journey was messed up, but it turned out to be the best thing to open my eyes about life. What is important is recognizing that **yours is the best journey meant for you, and you should go on that journey towards fulfillment.** Fulfillment is not about perfection. It is about identifying your unique journey, accepting it, and transforming it into a happy and fulfilling life. You are the author of your life.

In the following few chapters, you will learn how to create different results in your life, both internal and external, using the power of the mind and energy.

CHAPTER 37
USE THE POWER OF YOUR MIND

You are the one causing your life to happen. It all starts with your thoughts. By understanding your thoughts and changing their patterns, you can create the life you love. To do that, you have to **be conscious of your thoughts**. You have to see what thoughts are generated and clear non-productive thoughts. You have the ability to stop non-productive thought chains.

If you record your thoughts for one whole day, you will see what is happening inside your head. It is reflected in the current state of your life. See how much of your thoughts are related to Thought Bugs and how many are related to what matters to your life. There is no such thing as a mind recorder, but you can get the ability to see your thoughts through your higher consciousness. When you practice mindfulness, you can observe your thoughts.

RANDOM THOUGHTS

A person who does not have awareness creates random thoughts based on what is happening in their environment, including news and social media. Cravings, fear, self-limiting beliefs, and survival influence the thoughts. Those thoughts are not impactful in creating the life they desire.

INTENTION-LED THOUGHTS

To create a successful life, you need to drive your thoughts and energy via intentions. Intention-led thoughts carry an immense amount of creative energy.

Setting intentions will help you find your direction toward your desired life for each domain, like a global positioning system. Once you set the intention, you get thoughts on how to go to the desired results. That is the power of the human mind.

THE MIND

The mind is crucially responsible for your happiness, and having a conceptual picture to visualize your mind will help you understand it better. During my research, the best diagram I came across was the stick-figure diagram for the mind created by Dr. Thurman Fleet in 1930. Since then many other renowned teachers have used it. This is a simplified conceptual view of the mind:

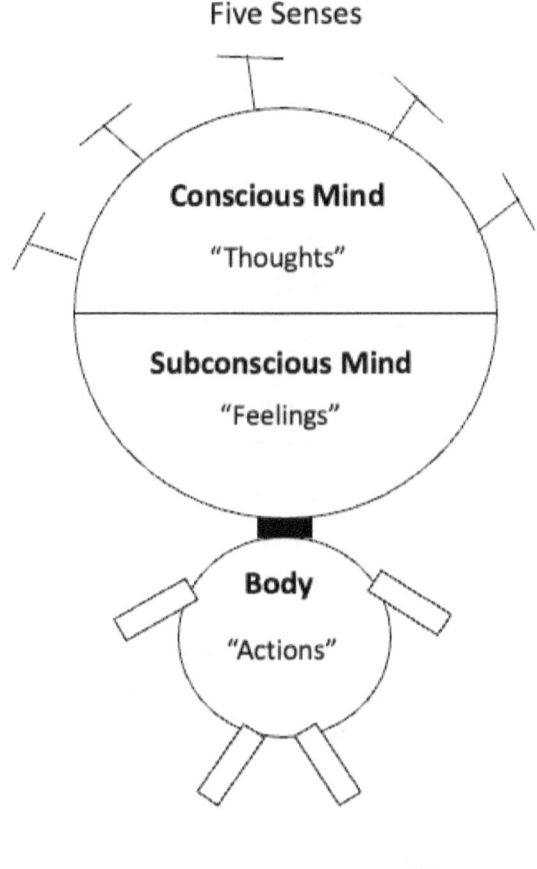

Conceptual Picture of the Mind

CONSCIOUS MIND

This is your thinking mind. Your thoughts are generated here. For example, you can consciously set intentions for your life domain. If you maintain a higher consciousness, you have higher control of your thoughts.

SUBCONSCIOUS MIND

The subconscious mind is where your feelings and emotions are generated. Your feelings are associated with your beliefs and past experiences.

If you are not aware enough, your subconscious mind will drive your thoughts, which are based on your current beliefs and feelings from past experiences. Past information is like old programs within you. They have been in your subconscious mind since childhood. For example, the Self-Limiting Thought Bug is one of these old programs. Re-programming the mind means that you plant new beliefs and experiences in your subconscious mind so that your direction of life starts changing from old behaviors to new.

BODY

The subconscious mind drives your body to act. Now think about going to the gym. Observe your feelings. Do they cause you to move your body and take action? If you have had great experiences at the gym in the past, positive feelings will be generated and your vibration will direct you to go the gym. Otherwise, your feelings will send signals to diminish your desire to go.

There is a way to influence your subconscious mind to influence your actions. You learned about dopamine as a neurotransmitter. If you can trigger dopamine, your feelings will change and you will get motivated. Setting intentions and visualizing the reward will motivate you with a dopamine hit. With dopamine, you can overwrite your old feelings, which will make you move. Be sure to make happy experiences, so that the next time your subconscious mind will move you with ease.

HOW TO CREATE NEW OUTCOMES

Sometimes you have great ideas and cannot create results. The main reason is that, until you align your subconscious mind with believing the idea and taking action, your energy is not effectively creating the matter in the world. This diagram shows how you can cause a new outcome in your life using energy:

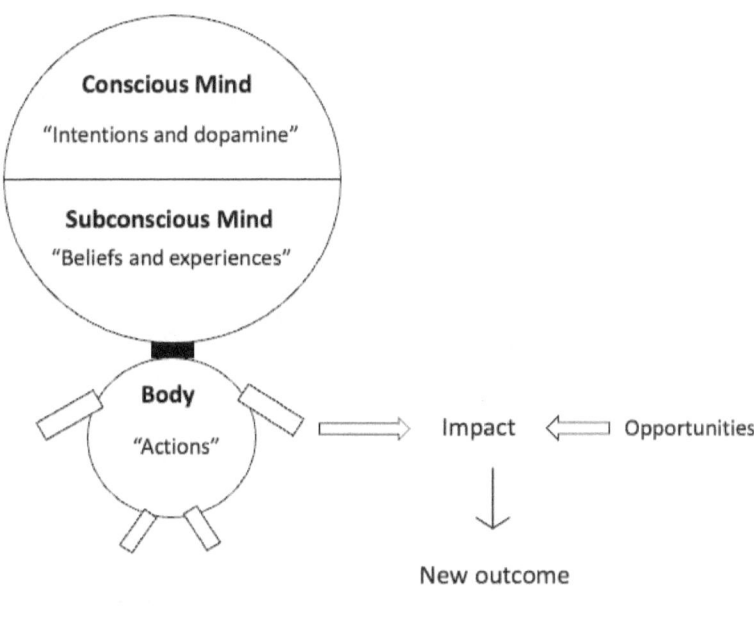

How to Create a New Outcome

Your subconscious mind moves you to action. **Once the subconscious mind believes in something, you can direct your energy to move to action.** If you make happy experiences, the subconscious mind remembers those happy feelings and drives you to do similar activities.

Now let's look at Happiness Mountain's power to create process, which is based on the conscious and subconscious mind and how they can drive you to take actions to fulfill different domains of your life.

POWER TO CREATE

Power to create is the systematic methodology to create new outcomes for your domains of the Life Fulfillment Map. It all starts with setting your intentions with your conscious mind:

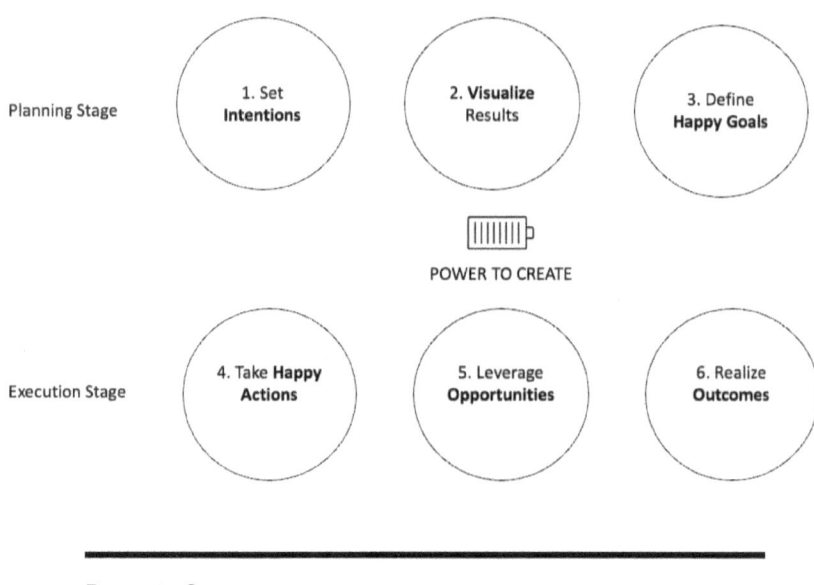

Power to Create

Here is a brief overview of each step:

1. **Set intentions:** For each life domain, define what you want.
2. **Visualization:** Visualize the outcome so that you get motivated with dopamine.

3. **Define goals:** What is the difference between an intention and a goal? The goal has a set timeline and measurable results, which may not be part of an intention. Goals will give focus to your mind to achieve a measurable outcome.
4. **Take happy actions:** Life is a journey. These actions are a part of it. Enjoy the actions as happy experiences. Make every experience a happy experience. Continue to maintain dopamine.
5. **Take new opportunities:** Only when you take actions will you will see new opportunities showing up. Notice incoming opportunities and accept them.
6. **New outcome:** You create a new outcome for your life domain with happiness.

HOW TO ACHIEVE GOALS HAPPILY

We all have hopes and goals in our lives. Goals make you feel alive. Goals help you to get the best out of your valuable human life.

As human beings, we want to archive our goals with desires. Whether these goals are small or big, we want expected results, and those become our expectations.

Someone who has not followed the Happiness Mountain methodology could set their goals with cravings, comparisons, fear, self-limiting beliefs, and worrying. Goals are associated with Negative Thought Bugs. One who goes after goals with Thought Bugs tends to suffer from them. If they achieve their goals, they are still not fulfilled and need more, with greediness. They would get sadness, anger, and judgments if they didn't reach the desired results. Negative Thought Bugs will make them stressed while pursuing goals.

Happiness Mountain's approach is to make every experience a happy experience. The goals should not have an attachment to Negative Thought Bugs. To do that, you should practice living with full positive energy, stop the Negative Thought Bugs, and live in the present moment with mindfulness. You can go further and connect to your Higher Self while pursuing your goals. For example, you associate your goals with your service in this world, experience the goal achievement process objectively, understand the impermanence, and always stay grounded by taking care of your mind and body. Give gratitude daily and be grateful for what you already have.

Use goals as a tool to keep you on track and focused. When you pursue goals with the right mindset, you always win, irrespective of the outcome. No matter the outcome, you will enjoy the experience and who you become by pursuing your goals.

THREE-STEP GOALS

You can also follow the three-step goal process that I follow:

1. **Easy Goal:** Start with an easy goal and start actioning. Begin with less expectations to get started; e.g., I set my 10K run with a 120-minute goal.
2. **Reasonable Goal:** Only after getting start will you get confidence and clarity. When you have clarity, you can define your goal better and make it a reasonable one; e.g., after practicing, I got more confidence to make a 90-minute goal to run 10K.
3. **Ideal Goal:** When you prepare for over 80 percent of the goal, you can set your target goal more clearly; e.g., I set my 10K run to be 75 minutes. I finished the 10K in 73 minutes.

SUCCESS

Success generally means getting the desired results for each domain. In some cases, there could be constraints for certain domains that you cannot get ideal results with. Then you can focus on becoming fulfilled with what you have. That, again, is success.

In Happiness Mountain, we focus on becoming fulfilled. Do not compare your life to others'. You can successfully fulfill a domain in other ways than you defined. Your conscious pursuit of a domain is a success. Your intentions, effort, and who you become while pursuing it is part of your success. There is no such thing as failure. Everything in life is a learning experience. Inner success is always in your hands. With inner success, you become strong and resilient.

External things are not always in your control. You can influence them but not control them. Therefore, define a significant part of your success based on the fulfillment of the journey toward your goals. For example, I have a goal to be a *New York Times* bestselling author so that happiness can be widespread around the world. Taking actions as happy experiences to become a bestselling author is a success for me. The outcome is not necessarily in my hands; I manifest and act as a *Times* bestselling author. I always create internal success and live happily and fulfilled while paving the path to external success.

HOW TO APPLY THE POWER TO CREATE

Let's look at how you can apply the power to create for differ life domains. I will use myself as the example.

DOMAIN: MIND

Intention: I want to live a happy and fulfilled life every single day.
Visualization: I visualize living on Happiness Mountain:

- I make every experience a happy experience.
- I am full of positive energy.
- I stop stressing and worrying.

- I live a joyful and balanced life.
- I maintain my inner happiness.
- I feel my greatness.
- I live a fulfilled life with happiness, health, and wealth.

Happy goals

- Read a chapter of the the Happiness Mountain Book before going to bed.
- Practice Happiness Mountain daily with the Happiness Mountain app.
- Continuous personal development with Happiness Mountain.

Happy actions

- Make every experience a happy experience in daily life.
- Track them with the app to keep myself conscious.

Opportunities

- Find peace at home and work.
- Increase self-love.
- Find life purpose.
- Make a difference in the world.

New Results: Living a truly happy and fulfilled life.

DOMAIN: BODY

Intention: Improve health, become active and feel good about my body.

Visualization: I imagine my active, healthy, and lean body.
Happy goals:

- One moderate to intense physical activity a day, producing endorphins.
- Daily stretching as soon as I wake up.
- Daily outdoor walk.
- Drink two liters of water daily.
- Strength exercises, twice a week.
- Yoga twice a week.
- Swimming two to three times a week.
- Sauna every other day.
- Maintain weight 135–140 lbs.
- Check blood every six months and make sure glucose and cholesterol are within the healthy range.
- Meet nutritionist two times a year and adjust eating habits.
- Use wearable tracker and check heart rate zones, calories, steps, and sleep quality.

Happy Actions

- Make every experience a happy experience when engaging my goals achieving activities.

Opportunities

- More energy during the day to do more things.
- Feel more confident with an enhanced mood.
- Self-love.

New outcome: Active, healthy, and lean body. I love it.

DOMAIN: GIVEBACK

Intention: Launch the book on my fiftieth birthday.

Visualization: Become a *New York Times* bestseller. Feels good about being able to create a new definition for happiness to the world.

Happy Goals

- Complete the book and share with the world on my fiftieth birthday
- Book launch event in October
- Become a *New York Times* bestselling author by 2025

Actions

- Make the book—writing, publishing, and launching—a happy experience.

Opportunities

- Speaker engagements, income from book sales

New Results: Happiness definition, philosophy and methodology created in the world. I became a *New York Times* bestselling author. (At the time of writing, this has not happened.)

Now it's your turn to pick your three priority domains and write your intentions and goals following the power to create process. You can download the workbook from happinessmountain.com/book/resources, or use the Happiness Mountain app to write them.

33 PERCENT THOUGHTS-ACTION FORMULA

Say you want to focus on improving a particular domain. It could be improving your mind, body or wealth. The simple formula I use is the thoughts-actions formula. My experience is that if you want to succeed in a particular area, you have to create at least one third (33 percent) of your thoughts and actions on any given day, especially at the beginning.

Monitor your thoughts with consciousness. Reduce wondering time. To get focus, you need at least 33 percent of your energy directed to your area of improvement.

Intention-led thoughts + Action = 33 percent energy

Intention
Healthy, active body

Intention led thoughts

- Healthy eating thoughts
- Learning biology basics (e.g., listening to a podcast)
- Finding activity classes
- Talk to friends to do activities with
- Adjusting daily schedule to accommodate time

Actions

For great results, this must be 33 percent or more of your thoughts during your time awake. Create and read affirmations in the morning and nighttime.

- Buying, preparing, and eating healthy food
- Joining physical activity classes
- Activities: swimming, yoga, running, walking, basketball, soccer, etc.

33 percent of thoughts resulted in many actions, which could lead to 33 percent of your energy.

CLEARING YOUR ENERGY BLOCKS

The primary blocker that someone can face is that they have an idea in the conscious mind but their subconscious mind contains a conflicting belief. You may have noticed that sometimes you set intentions and they do not work for you. When you set intentions, **look deep inside your subconscious mind to see what you believe.**

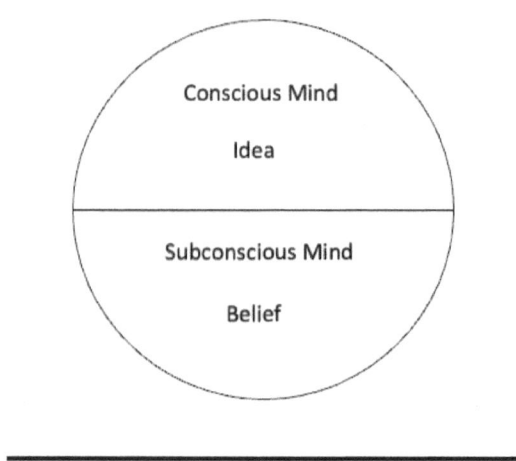

Aligning Conscious and Subconscious Minds

When ideas and beliefs are not aligned within the mind, there is a conflict and your power to create is significantly impacted.

Let's take an example—say I want to lose ten pounds. At the same time, I love eating out and all types of food. Love for food is in the subconscious. A new idea for losing weight is my New Year's resolution. Now they are conflicting. In this case, either you have to set a more powerful belief into your subconscious, overwriting the original belief, or accept that you love food and are not too concerned about losing weight by dieting. Instead, come up with a new idea, which is to increase exercise and enjoy food simultaneously. As you can now see, the idea is in line with the belief. Therefore, you become happier since there is no conflict.

When you are coming up with an idea and want to realize it, it is imperative to cross-check and understand your subconscious beliefs to make sure they are aligned. Otherwise, you cannot fully execute your absolute power to create while you have an energy block. You have to **flow your energy freely from the conscious to the subconscious to action**. Then you feel great, and you start seeing results with ease.

Sometimes you have to be conscious that your overall life may have energy blocks. For example, you create something unique to create new results in life. At the same time, you are going through a relationship issue. Now the relationship issue is an energy block. Your conscious mind may say "I want a great loving relationship," but your subconscious mind may say "my partner does not love me." You need to resolve this common mismatch to allow your energy to flow freely. My advice is to follow Happiness Mountain, and your relationships will become great. I have seen positive changes in relationships in my life and in those of many others who climbed Happiness Mountain. Focus on being a good human being and work on defeating Negative Thought Bugs. Do not judge other people; look inside and work on your mind. There are other tools, like relationship counseling. Seek help and create understanding to remove negative energy blocks in your life. This is essential to creating a happy, healthy, and wealthy life.

WINS

Celebrate your wins. Get dopamine joy by changing your mindset to see the wins toward the goal as achievements, even when the wins are small. Make wins every day toward your goals and be happy!

CHAPTER 38

USE THE POWER OF ENERGY

L ife is all about energy. When you want to fulfill an area of your life, take advantage of energy. You learned about the physical universe and the energetic universe in Happiness Experience Four. Let me remind you of the diagram:

The Universe

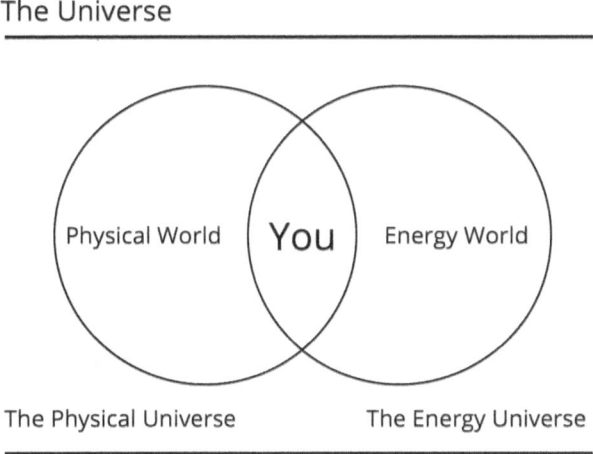

The Physical Universe   The Energy Universe

The physical world's matter is created from energy. By understanding energy, you can create what matters in your life. Human beings have the great power to create matter from energy, which other living beings such as dogs or cats do not have. You got the highest form of living from with power to create matter in this world. Let's activate your power and create a happy and fulfilling life.

THREE ENERGY LAWS

How do you understand energy better? There are three basic energy laws that you will learn in Happiness Mountain:

1. **Law of Vibration:** This is the energy from your vibration.
2. **Law of Creation:** This is how you create what matters to you in life using energy.
3. **Law of Attraction:** This is how you attract other energies to support your creations.

LAW OF VIBRATION

> Everything in life is vibration.
>
> – Albert Einstein

You have a vibration. Based on how you think and feel, your vibration changes. The ideal way to manage energy is to reduce the mind's wandering and keep your mind focused on what matters to you. **If you can maintain intensity of focus, you will have more power to create.** If you are excessively wondering, you will have less ability to create matter in the physical world.

The following diagram shows how I manage my energy states by observing my consciousness. My target is to maintain 80 percent non-mind-wandering time.

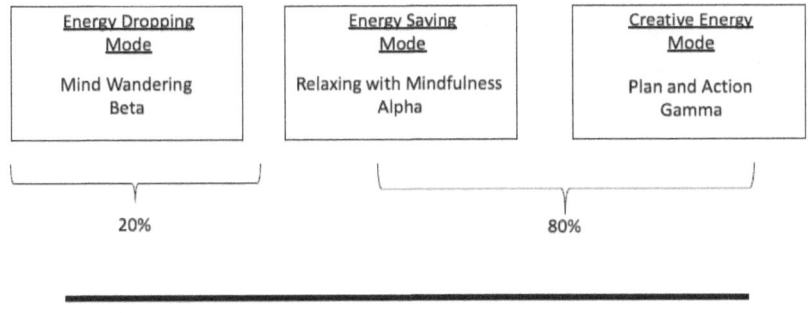

Three States of Mind

ENERGY MODES

- **Energy-dropping mode:** Energy is dropped by wandering, being busy, and by Negative Thought Bugs. Avoid drenching the brain in the high beta waves we learned about in in the Mindfulness chapter.
- **Energy-saving mode:** Practice mindfulness to save energy. Use the feelings from the five senses and stay in the present moment. If you go for a walk, mindfully do so without going into thought chains. Feel the air touching your skin. Observe what is around you but do not add meaning to it. Practice mindfully relaxing throughout the day, including taking intermittent breaks from work. This is your alpha brain-wave range.
- **Creative-energy mode:** This is where you focus on your intentions and goals. Use all your saved energy to work on what matters to you. This is the gamma range of the

brain. Creative work in the early morning helps bring you to high-concentration zones.

Let's call your energy related to vibration "Life Energy." By climbing the first five experiences of Happiness Mountain, you now have a higher Life Energy.

To work with energy laws effectively, you must be at a higher vibration, which you get from the previous five happiness experiences. If you skip them, I recommend working on them and getting your Life Energy to a higher vibration. You do not have to be perfect, but you need awareness and daily practice. For example, you must recognize Thought Bugs to stop your energy dropping while achieving goals. You need Happy Hormones to keep the motivation to do the actions. You need your Higher Self to maintain your Inner Happiness no matter how big the goal is. With a higher vibration, everything becomes readily achievable.

People who suffer while trying to achieve goals are the ones who have not increased their vibration. Then they give up their plans. Some people appear to be successful from the outside, but they are not happy inside. They have not increased their vibration, but they have gained material things which can make them suffer internally.

Practice Happiness Mountain daily to stay in a higher vibration.

LAW OF CREATION

$$L^B \times A = O$$

L = Life energy
  B = Believe

A = Action
O = Outcome

I created the above Law of Creation for the Happiness Mountain methodology.

Life Energy (L)

As noted in the Law of vibration, your Life Energy is key to accomplishing goals in life that matter to you. If you want to achieve something, you need to bring a matching vibration to what you want to accomplish. Your vibration affects what you believe. Based on your Life Energy, the following will happen:

- A higher vibration allows you to see your path clearly.
- With higher vibration, you can believe in yourself.
- Higher vibrations help you to believe in bigger goals.
- With higher vibration, you can accomplish what matters in life efficiently.
- With higher vibrations, you can attract good things in life.

Belief (B)

Believing in yourself and that you can accomplish what matters to you gives you the greatest power. Belief magnifies your energy exponentially. With a high Life Energy (L) and Belief (B), you will have immense energy to take actions.

- Believe in yourself.
- Believe in the outcome you want.

- Believe in the actions that will take you to the desired outcome.
- Believe in a higher power.
- Believe in others who support you.

Say you have a high vibration, but you do not believe that it is for something you want. Your Belief (B) is small, and you can't energize such a goal with your Life Energy. You will have to adjust your goal to something you believe that you want to accomplish. When you believe and do, you are happy. When you do something happily, you have higher changes of success.

Belief is part of subconscious mind. The best way to establish the belief is visualization and affirmation. The more you visualize, the more your subconscious mind starts believing it is real.

Power of Affirmations

Affirmations change your subconscious beliefs so that your thoughts and actions are directed toward your goals.

"Who Am I" Script

This is where you read an affirmation as your futuristic self as if it has already happened. To change your vibration, you have to think like the person you want to be. The formula is "be, do, have." To take advantage of the Law of Vibration and the Law of Attraction, you have to think you are already the person that you want to be. You have to visualize and become that person in the energetic universe, and get all the energies you want to create the state in the physical universe.

Here is an example from my "who am I" script:

• • •

I am Amal Indi. My purpose is to make the world a happier place by inspiring and empowering people to stop suffering from thoughts and becoming happier and more fulfilled.

I am an author, speaker, and transformational leader in the world. I am the founder and CEO of Happiness Mountain. I am fulfilled with everything and everyone in my life: loving kids, a loving family, a loving partner, uplifting friends, mentors, a great leadership team, accountants, a legal firm, publishers, developers, and animators, and I am focusing on healing people happily.

Happiness Mountain has millions of subscribers around the world and generates millions of dollars to make more goodness in the world. I always take care of my mind-body first, with a higher consciousness. I am whole and complete. I live a fulfilled life with happiness, health, and wealth doing what I love.

I read it daily before going to the bed. The more I read it and visualize the outcome, the more my subconscious mind believes that it is real. With a higher belief, I have immense energy to take actions and materialize the outcome in the physical world.

I started with a simple script and enhanced it over time. Please create your script and read it before bed and as soon as you wake up, so that it goes to your subconscious mind and changes your vibration.

I also read belief affirmations, such as:

- I am smart and intelligent enough to achieve anything I want.
- I am attracting more and more abundance simply by being the great person I am.
- I am a loving and conscious person who is making a difference in the world.

- I live in an abundant universe, and money always comes to me easily and effortlessly.

Now it's your turn to create a "who am I" script with your ideal life and affirmations to empower you to achieve it.

Action (A)

With a higher vibration, by believing in what you want to achieve, and taking action courageously, you can access massive energy from the energetic universe and create what matters in your life.

Without actions, nothing will happen. Some people believe they can achieve a goal but they do not act. Say you want career advancement and higher pay. You need to update your résumé and apply for the next level of the job that you love. Taking no action means that nothing will change, even if you believe you can do it and have the right energy.

You must believe in your actions. If you do not believe in one action, find one that you believe in.

Outcome (O)

Shoot for the moon. Even if you miss, you'll land among the stars.

— Norman Vincent Peale

Dream big. Follow the power-to-create process. The energetic universe has abundant energy for you to take and create the life you love.

LAW OF ATTRACTION

You have to ask what you want in life. The same principle applies with the universe. You have to ask the universe for what you want. When you ask the universe, you receive opportunities to get what you ask for. How do you ask the universe? I use three methods:

DIRECT ASK

- Dear Universe, show me the path to [what you want], and many, many years to come.
- Dear Universe, show me the path to becoming a *New York Times* bestselling author, and many, many years to come.

BELIEF AFFIRMATION

Write your goal-achieving affirmations and "who am I" script. Goal achieving affirmations look like this:

- I am happy and grateful now that I am a *New York Times* bestselling author.
- I am happy and grateful now that the Happiness Mountain book sold over a million copies.

VISION BOARD

With a vision board, you can have pictures and text describing your future self and goals that you want to achieve. For example, I have a picture of my book with "*New York Times* bestselling book" on the cover. My son created a vision board with the picture of the university he wants to attend.

The Law of Attraction is when you attract people and opportunities based on your vibration and what you ask for, a.k.a. manifest.

Reading these belief affirmations daily keeps me motivated with dopamine and creates energy attractions in the energetic universe to easily achieve the goal. For example, I meet the right people to achieve the goal. I started seeing new opportunities that aligned with the outcome I manifested. And I know when I see an opportunity to take action with. Remember the fifth step of the Power to Create process: "Take new opportunities." Since I am in a higher consciousness, I can see the opportunity quickly. If my mind throws me a thought that it won't work, I know how to ignore it, since I know it is a Self-Limiting Thought Bug.

When you manifest with a higher vibration and believe in the outcome, it starts being realized in the physical universe. You convert energy in the energetic universe to matter in the physical universe.

POWER TO CREATE WITH ENERGY LAWS

> Imagination is more important than knowledge. For knowledge is limited, whereas imagination embraces the entire world, stimulating progress, giving birth to evolution.
>
> —ALBERT EINSTEIN

HAPPINESS MOUNTAIN

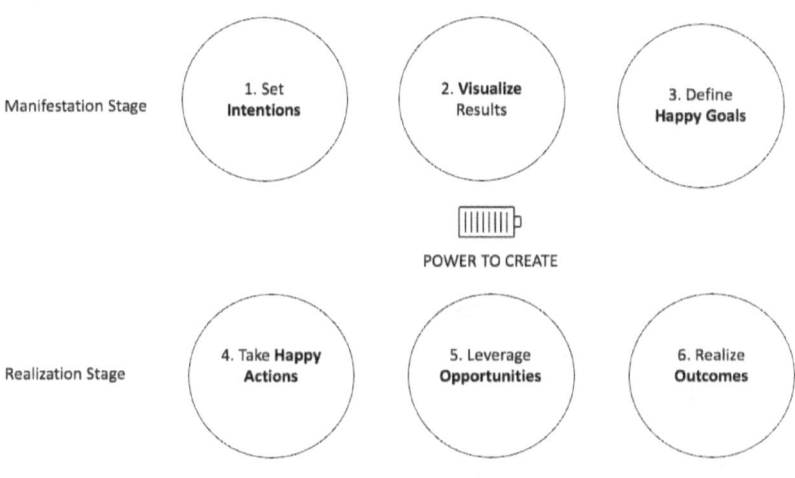

Power to Create

- **Manifestation stage:** This is where you manifest and organize the energy from the energetic universe for your intention. There is a massive amount of fresh energy in the universe for you to take.
- **Realization stage:** Realization is where you are creating outcomes you want in the physical world. Realization starts with actions, and everything is waiting for your action in the physical world to attract and realize the outcome. Trust that the energy is ready for you and take courageous actions during this stage. Nothing can stop you.

Let's look at each step of power to create process from an energy-laws point of view:

1. **Set intentions:** Manifest what you want and change your vibration. You initiate an energy change in the universe. Your brain will generate messages within you with dopamine neurotransmitters.
2. **Visualization:** When you visualize, your vibration changes and attracts necessary energies. You start believing firmly in visualization. It would help if you created a daily affirmation and read it while imagining the new experience. Please write it as if it has already happened (e.g., "I am happy and grateful now that I am a *New York Times* bestselling author"). I visualize the Happiness Mountain book on the *Times*' bestselling list. The feelings in your subconscious mind change, and you emit these new energy message signals to the universe. Your intensity of neurotransmitter messages within you also gets intensified with dopamine. The more you believe and visualize, the more energy and dopamine intensity increase.
3. **Define goals:** Define timelines and measurements of the outcome and give more clarity to it. When you have more clarity, your mind will efficiently direct you to the outcome.
4. **Take happy actions:** You must take action to realize outcomes in the physical world. The more power you have from intentions, visualizations, and goal-setting, the more energy you have to take action powerfully. Your mind, body, and energy in the universe are all ready for your actions. Courageously take action. Do not listen to your self-limiting beliefs. Trust yourself and the universe and do it.
5. **Take new opportunities:** You start attracting new opportunities supporting your outcome from the Law of Attraction. Stay alert to the opportunities. Take them without doubting. Be courageous and take action. If you

get a thought with an opportunity, act on it immediately. Those moments are energetic. Do not overthink and wait to do it later. Do it right away. Some of those thoughts might be bigger than your current state. Go for them, trusting the universe, irrespective of how big or small they are. Start listening to the messages coming to your mind from the higher powers in the universe.

6. **New Outcome:** New matter is created from your energy combined with the other energies from the universe.

SELF-DISCIPLINE

To create a new outcome takes time. Keep your vibration up until you achieve the goal by:

- **Self-control:** The ability to manage one's impulses, emotions, and behaviors to achieve long-term goals.
- **Willpower:** The ability to resist short-term gratification in pursuit of long-term goals or objectives.
- **Self-concentration:** The ability to direct one's thinking in whatever direction one would intend.

Now you have the necessary knowledge to attain Happiness Experience Six: Life Fulfillment with happiness, health, and wealth, doing what you love. Write your intentions for each life domain of Life Fulfillment Map. Start with intentions and prioritize one domain with full power-to-create process. Make sure you always live by the core philosophy of Happiness Mountain while you are fulfilling your domains.

Make every experience a happy experience

Conclusion: Make the World a Happier Place

CHAPTER 39
LIVING ON HAPPINESS MOUNTAIN

Congratulations! By reading and completing the practices, you have conquered Happiness Mountain. Continue to stay on the journey of every happy experience. Now you have the manual for your happy life. Go back to the appropriate chapters whenever you forget, fall off, or get stuck. These are practices to do every day until they become your new way of life, your new mindset. If you are not doing this, you are choosing a different mindset, and it is not serving you or giving you the true happiness you want. Now you have all the necessary tools. Re-read it and re-do the practices. You will always find areas for improvement. Happiness Mountain practices are for your whole life. Keep practicing every day; eventually, you will be able to do it without thinking about it. You are reprogramming your mind. You are recreating your life. Here are a few things you can do next.

CLIMB AGAIN

Climb Happiness Mountain again. The hardest time is the first. You don't notice everything when you climb the first time. When you climb Happiness Mountain for the second time, you will feel more joy and see things you overlooked the first time. Make Happiness Mountain practices your way of life! You will start discovering more happiness, greatness, and fulfillment each time you climb.

SHARE YOUR GREATNESS

You are unique. You are awesome. You are happy. You have the power to create a greater purpose and lead a transformational life. Be the best version of yourself.

SHARE YOUR LOVE

Share your journey up to Happiness Mountain with others. Tell them about your great discoveries. Spread love and happiness. You can share Happiness Mountain with your family, friends, work colleagues, community, and anyone you think can help to become happier in their life. You never know who you will influence to climb Happiness Mountain!

MAKE THE WORLD A HAPPIER PLACE

If all of us individually live on Happiness Mountain and make every experience a happy experience, we all make the world a happier place. Brighten the world with your greatness!

REVIEW REQUEST

Thank you so much for taking this journey with me. Your time and interest are genuinely appreciated. I hope this book has offered you insights, made you think, or simply brought you joy.

If it did, would you consider taking a few moments to share your thoughts? Your review not only means a lot to me personally – yes, I read every single one – but it also plays a crucial role in helping others discover this book. Your unique perspective can guide potential readers who might be wondering if this book is for them.

Just visit the platform where you purchased the book, and leave a review there. It doesn't need to be lengthy – a sentence or two is perfect.

Thank you once again for your time and support. It truly means the world to me!

NOTES

1. HAPPINESS DEFINITION

1. "Happiness." Merriam-Webster.com. 2022. https://www.merriam-webster.com (17 July 2022).

15. EIGHT THOUGHT BUGS®: TRIGGERS OF NEGATIVE ENERGY

1. "Craving." Merriam-Webster.com. 2022. https://www.merriam-webster.com (17 July 2022).

23. SELF-LIMITING THOUGHT BUG

1. https://dictionary.cambridge.org/dictionary/english/trauma?q=Trauma (21 Aug 2022)

26. HOW TO CREATE A JOYFUL & BALANCED LIFE

1. Excerpted from the https://www.health.harvard.edu/mind-and-mood/feel-good-hormones-how-they-affect-your-mind-mood-and-body, July, 2021© copyright Harvard University.

27. DOPAMINE = MOTIVATION + DRIVE + PLEASURE

1. https://www.health.harvard.edu/mind-and-mood/dopamine-the-pathway-to-pleasure (28 Dec 2022)

33. CONNECT TO YOUR HIGHER SELF

1. https://www.mindtools.com/pages/article/authenticity.htm (16 Oct 2022)
2. https://hbr.org/2013/10/be-yourself-but-carefully (30 Dec 2022)

NOTES

35. YOUR NINE GIVEBACKS

1. NOAA. Ten Simple Things You Can Do to Help Protect the Earth
    National Ocean Service website, https://oceanservice.noaa.gov/ocean/earth-day.html, access on 04/09/23.

Acknowledgments

I sincerely thank everyone who helped me to bring this book to life. I extend my deepest gratitude and thanks to the following:

Mom and Dad - I dedicate this book to you! Without you, I would not be where I am today. (I wish Dad could have celebrated the release of this book with us, but he has passed away.) Thank you, Mom and Dad, for all your effort in raising me and your guidance in showing me how to be a good person in the world.

My children Tehan and Ethan - Your patience and unwavering support during the times I couldn't be fully present while working on Happiness Mountain are deeply appreciated. Your understanding means the world to me, and your dad is truly thankful for both of you!

My ex-wife Dilani - You offered unwavering support throughout the process of completing the book. Your backing was crucial in enabling me to complete Happiness Mountain with peace of mind. Thank you for your invaluable support.

Lahiru Munasinghe - Thank you for your dedication and hard work in bringing the Happiness Mountain App to life alongside the book. You've been an integral part of the Happiness Mountain journey from its inception, consistently offering your unwavering positive energy and support along the way.

Julie Howgate - Thank you for serving as my advisor and providing invaluable guidance on communication matters. Your strong dedication to Happiness Mountain means a lot to me.

Simon Ogden - Thank you for your exceptional and insightful substantive edits that have truly elevated the book's quality.

Jack Canfield - Your endorsement of Happiness Mountain, words of encouragement, and valuable guidance have been instrumental in my journey.

I am grateful to all my family, friends, teachers, advisers, mentors, coaches, and spiritual leaders who have helped me in this long journey of creating Happiness Mountain. Thank you for your constant inspiration and support.

Amal Indi, 2023

ABOUT THE AUTHOR

After spending over 20 years in the technology and corporate banking sectors, Amal Indi created The Happiness Mountain™ to help people reach their peak of happiness.

Happiness Mountain® introduces innovative methodology, philosophy, techniques, and tools to boost happiness. These resources are strategically designed to enrich personal, professional, and spiritual realms, fostering holistic well-being.

Amal's aspirations extend to healing the world by enabling people to access genuine happiness, irrespective of their backgrounds. Amal believes that if we all live individually on Happiness Mountain, we all make the world a happier place. Amal is also a father of two children and lives in beautiful Vancouver, Canada.

facebook.com/onhappymountain
linkedin.com/company/happinessmountain
instagram.com/onhappymountain
tiktok.com/@onhappymountain
youtube.com/@HappinessMountain.Official

ALSO BY AMAL INDI

THE AUTHORITIES - LIFE ENERGY

by Amal Indi (Author), Les Brown (Author), Raymond Aaron (Author), Marci Shimoff (Author), Dr Nido Qubein (Foreword)

This marks Amal's inaugural book, co-authored alongside three esteemed *New York Times* bestselling writers. The Authorities - Life Energy book is available on Amazon.

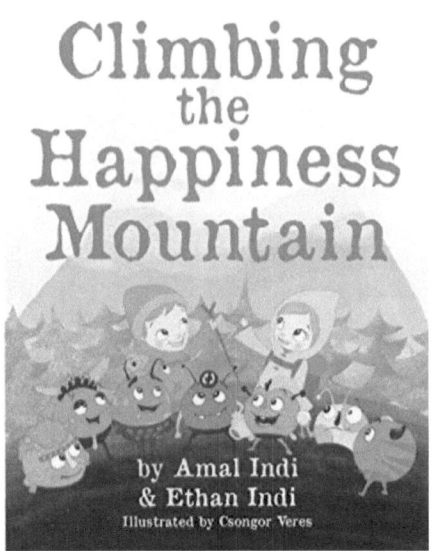

CLIMBING THE HAPPINESS MOUNTAIN

by Amal Indi (Author), Ethan Indi (Author), Csongor Veres (Illustrator)

Amal co-authored *Climbing the Happiness Mountain* children's book with his son, Ethan.

Climbing the Happiness Mountain is a wonderful book that teaches children self-esteem, acceptance, patience, gratification, and courage. By focusing on positive thoughts children learn how to deal with negative emotions.

Ted and Mia go on an adventure climbing the Happiness Mountain. On the way, they meet anger bug that is really upset because it's camping gear has been stolen. Ted and Mia help the anger bug to clam down. Ted says to Anger bug what he does is repeat 3 times "I am calm and relaxed". This helps the anger bug to calm down. On the adventure, they meet low self-esteem bug, suspicion bug, judgmental bug, procrastination bug, obsession bug, and worry bug.

Happiness Mountain is beautifully illustrated with vivid colors that children can easily identify with and remember. Get your copy from Amazon!

Happiness Mountain App
FOR YOUR DAILY HAPPINESS

Embark on a rewarding journey with the Happiness Mountain App. It's designed to guide your learning, foster your practice, and visually track your progress as you ascend the summit of happiness!

The Happiness Mountain App is coming soon to the App Store and Google Play Store. Stay updated by registering for our newsletter at www.happinessmountain.com.

www.ingramcontent.com/pod-product-compliance
Lightning Source LLC
Chambersburg PA
CBHW030544080526
44585CB00012B/252